Breakfast in Princeton, USA

A Year-Long Odyssey
1996

Ken Perry

Breakfast in Princeton, USA
A Year-Long Odyssey—1996
Ken Perry
Tiger-50 Publishing

Published by Tiger-50 Publishing
Copyright ©2016 Ken Perry
All rights reserved.

Editor: Bill Motchan

Cover and Interior design: Davis Creative, www.DavisCreative.com

Front cover photo: Bill Motchan

Back cover photo: Ken Perry

All interior photos: Ken and Garie Perry

ISBN: 978-0-692-69712-2

2016

DEDICATION

*To the friendly folks who
called these Princetons their homes,
and welcomed us into their lives*

*Cover photo: Same car, same people
who took the 1996 trips in this book*

Table of Contents

Acknowledgments

There are more than a few who have contributed in different ways to bring this undertaking to a satisfying conclusion:

Bill Motchan who helped winnow my original 77,944 words, rigorously edited my manuscripts, catching flaws I was unaware of and making astute suggestions for much needed modifications

Jack Davis who skillfully prepared our photographs for print and devised a layout that truly reflects our odyssey

And the rest of "Team Princeton:"

Mary Chmielewicz who painstakingly proofed the final manuscript

Cathy Davis who smoothly handled the publishing arrangements

Jeff and Janet Rainford who started the ball rolling by recommending the team

Joshua, our black cat, who helped by shuffling selected papers and photos to the floor and lounging on my computer keyboard

And finally, Garie, my wife of 59 years and companion on the odyssey, who selected the photographs, offered valuable suggestions and proofed It was her persistence that finally convinced me to write this book.

Should there be errors or inaccuracies, they are of my doing.

"Follow your bliss."
--Joseph Campbell

I went to Princeton, the university in New Jersey, that is. I say this with some pride, being the first member of my family to complete college. I also owe a huge debt of gratitude for my college experience.

The genesis of this book, and the journey it catalogues, began in August 1995. My wife, Garie, and I were driving through Iowa toward Minnesota to visit her brother the day after our 38th wedding anniversary. We had spent our anniversary night at a bed and breakfast on an Iowa hog farm. This particular B & B had intrigued us when the host described the amenities. It did not have a Jacuzzi, but the package *did* include home cured bacon and a tour of the hog barns.

Much of our time after my 1985 retirement had been devoted to teaching and directing a program in China teaching English as a Second Language. After nine years, we had decided to take a break from China, but we had no specific plans. Why did the thought of visiting all the Princetons in the United States surface while we were somewhere in Iowa? Perhaps some stimulant at the hog farm triggered the recollection of a 1967 article in the *Princeton (University) Alumni Weekly* about 26 towns named "Princeton." (Our research eventually identified 32.)

While driving through Wisconsin, we saw a sign to "Princeton." Garie suggested we drive there. Rather than departing from our planned route, I countered that we wait and put together a larger "Princeton" plan. The ball started rolling a few days later when I mentioned to a friend that we might visit all the Princetons in the United States. That committed us to an odyssey the following year. Several months later over coffee at one of our favorite breakfast spots in Rockport, Massachusetts, we decided breakfast would be an integral part of each visit.

You may ask, as many of our friends have, why we undertook this venture. Certainly not because we wanted to emulate the cross-country travels of John Steinbeck or Charles Kuralt or William Least Heat Moon. It's noteworthy that 1996 was the 250th Anniversary of Princeton University, and this would be a unique way to commemorate its bicenquinquagenery year.

It's also worth considering a quote from Princeton's Hall of Fame basketball coach Pete Carril when he posed the question, "What fun is it to be Spanish and not chase your windmills?" When we proffered this explanation some friends asked if we were Spanish. No, but paraphrasing Carril's question gave a certain validity to our odyssey. "What fun is it to be a Princetonian and not visit Princetons?"

Garie's reply was probably the best. She simply quoted Joseph Campbell's advice to "follow your bliss."

So join us as we follow our bliss, blending exploration, history and anecdotes as we have "Breakfast in Princeton, USA."

Ken Perry
May 2016

TRIP #1

Missouri
Nebraska
Kansas

"Just don't show my backside."

...waitress at Griff's Korner Cafe

Princeton, Missouri
Population: 1,021
Breakfast for two: $6.80 plus tip

We left our St. Louis home in late January certain of only three things about Princeton, Missouri: that it actually existed and it had a post office and motel. We had talked to Mike Hickman, the postmaster, who not only made sure the Circle S Motel received their mail, but let them know we were coming.

A reassuring, slightly weathered sign greeted us on U.S. 65 near Wildcat Creek. It proclaimed Princeton, Missouri, as the birthplace of Calamity Jane (née Martha Jane Canary).

Kohl & Middleton's
PALACE MUSEUM
West Beginning Monday, Jan. 19.

CALAMITY JANE!

The Famous Woman Scout of the Wild West! Heroine of a Thousand Thrilling Adventures! The Terror of Evildoers in the Black Hills! The Comrade of Buffalo Bill and Wild Bill! See this Famous Woman and Hear Her Graphic Description of Her Daring Exploits!

A HOST OF OTHER ATTRACTIONS
Two Big Stage Shows!
that's all | ONE DIME! | that's all

There were few indications of life on this frigid day. Pick-up trucks dotted the snow-covered square, and an occasional man dressed for the elements in earflap hats, heavy khaki jackets, winter trousers and rubber boots walked by. A wall posting in the Circle S had informed us "It's a small town when the pick-up trucks outnumber the cars."

Our first Princeton definitely qualified as a small town.

The focal point of the town was the square situated on a ridge. It had a bandstand surrounded by a market, the Mercantile Bank with a digital thermometer apparently stuck on zero, a vacant storefront advertising Saturday auctions, the *Post-Telegraph* office, Wanda's Wear and Griff's Korner Cafe.

Next morning, we hailed a man crossing the square, who headed to Griff's. His name was Frank Buchtel. He was an affable 90-year-old, former teacher and coach who graciously removed his gloves to take our picture in front of the cafe. The three of us headed inside for a hot breakfast, the perfect answer to the blustery -41° wind chill.

The cafe had a few tables and ten booths with wood-backed seats and blue plastic upholstery. The cook sizzled sausage and flipped pancakes in a closed-off area. Lining the wall along the booths were a dozen sepia prints

of Old West good and bad guys and gals. They included hometown gal Calamity Jane.

Our waitress kept our coffee cups full. She was a short, ample woman by her own admission, and agreed to a photo with us with the admonition, "Just don't show my backside." It was an excellent country breakfast, though we passed up the biscuits and gravy.

The square comes alive in September when the annual Calamity Jane Days take place to commemorate "Princeton's most famous former citizen," despite the "less than perfect" reputation she established after leaving this northwest Missouri farmland. Evidently, Jane left the fledgling town in 1861 when she was ten years old. She never returned.

While at the square we stopped by the *Post Dispatch* office. Recognizing a story, Editor Preston Cole took our picture for an article, which appeared the next week under his byline as the front-page lead.

Breakfast was just one routine during our odyssey. Another was mailing a postcard picturing Nassau Hall from each Princeton to

Princeton University President Harold Shapiro. For good measure, we mailed one to ourselves. Mike, the postmaster, officially hand-stamped the Missouri cards.

We gassed up our '93 Buick Century just east off the square at a vintage filling station that also offered state vehicle inspections. The station had once been an integral part of the town but was gradually being displaced by Casey's market/self service station on the highway.

The pumps stood between white masonry columns that supported the canopy. No credit card, only cash. The barehanded attendant pumped the gas and flashed a smile as I paid.

We hit the road, west to Nebraska, remembering the genuinely friendly folks in our first Princeton. They had wished us well and told us that they hoped their Princeton would measure up to the others.

"We're wholesome people!"

...owner of the Princeton Tavern

Princeton, Nebraska
Population: 30
Breakfast for two: $7.50 plus tip

B risk winds blew snow across the road as we drove west from Missouri to Nebraska. At Beatrice (pronounced Be-AT-rice), we swung north on U.S. 77 toward Lincoln. All three waitresses at a McDonald's restaurant had heard of Princeton and thought it was on U.S. 77 south of Lincoln. They seriously doubted we would find a breakfast place there.

Just north of Beatrice on the horizon we saw the silhouette of a grain elevator, a sure indicator of a town. The four-lane highway abruptly narrowed to two lanes, where a white-on-green sign announced: "Princeton, Unincorporated." No population mentioned.

Years earlier, the town had a grocery and general merchandise store, a hardware store, a service station and its own post office. A few empty stores remained, along with a dozen houses and two unlikely neighbors—the Missionary Alliance Church and the Princeton Tavern. The last village black-

smith closed his shop and retired in 1971.

We approached the church and tavern and chose the latter to make our first contact. Sherry Snoad was behind the bar. She was the owner, proprietor, cook, accountant and handy person. Sherry also had a good memory. The following morning she recounted my first words, "This may sound strange but my wife and I are planning to visit all the Princetons in the United States."

The tavern was in a two-story, framed building on Main and Broad Streets, the latter gravel and 400 yards long. A collection of beer cans sat on shelves along two walls. The pool table bore a note stating children were not allowed to play. A snow-dusted beer garden was just outside. It was easy to visualize the garden on a hot summer evening, filled with customers from surrounding towns such as Sprague, Haltram and Firth, laughing and enjoying the weekend Mexican fare.

Sherry reckoned the population was about 30, which easily made it the smallest Princeton we would visit. She added, "It seemed like most of them lived in my house."

We also met the Hellers in the tavern. They had 600 acres of corn and soybeans. They expanded our knowledge of farming as they explained that their practice of no-till farming was especially good for "plateaued" areas. It did require more herbicides because the residual forage absorbed some of the liquid.

Two notable events had occurred recently in town. The 1930s-vintage brick Princeton State Bank building was relocated to the Nebraska State Fair Grounds. Then there was a Union Pacific train derailment. Both boosted tavern business for several months. Sherry knew her history and emphatically discounted local lore that Jesse James once robbed the bank. She was right. It turns out James died in 1882, 14 years before Princeton was founded.

Sherry gave us a breakfast menu and a screaming orange baseball/hunting cap with "Princeton Tavern" emblazoned in black above a game-cock. A smaller inscription below proclaimed "Home of the Big Cocks."

The orange caps (priced at $6) were popular in hunting season. Her stock was running low and the script in the forthcoming order would be limited to "Princeton Tavern." The pastor of neighboring Missionary Alliance Church would likely approve.

Overnight, the late January temperature reached -16°. Next morning, we happily stepped into the tavern's warmth. The coffee came fast, both regular and decaf. A woman at the bar said she was going to H&R Block to take care of "that thing." Sherry moaned, pointed to a box of expense records on the bar awaiting preparation of her tax returns, and retreated to the kitchen to prepare breakfast orders.

As we took our leave, well fed and warm, Sherry gave us big hugs. We had been total strangers less than 24 hours earlier. Now we were friends with the common bond of Princeton. We drove south to Kansas and savored Sherry's apt description of the tavern clientele: "We're wholesome people!"

"Did you know the healing power of emu oil?"

...a local realtor

Princeton, Kansas
Population: 275
Breakfast for two (and postmaster): $2 plus postmaster's coffee

You could easily miss the exit for Princeton, Kansas, if you didn't slow down on U.S. 59 south of Ottawa. We did. There were few signs of life along the one-mile stretch of road where the town officially began and ended between the familiar white-on-green "CITY LIMIT" signs. There was one business enterprise: a no-frills liquor store.

The one-mile square town began in the 1860s when the Leavenworth, Lawrence & Galveston railroad built a rail siding. Local legend suggested that Quantrill's Raiders ravaged the nearby countryside during the Civil

War. Princeton was likely a thriving farm community in the early 1900s. During our visit, it was primarily a bedroom community for neighboring towns. Its residents lived in a mix of old and new, modest frame houses and mobile homes. Vacant storefronts and the remnants of a vintage filling station with two ancient pumps and glass cylinders were evidence of the town's past. Electronic seed counters made in a new prefabbed building held hope for its future.

We entered the post office to find 140 numbered, brass dial-and-pointer mailboxes. Here's where townsfolk came to collect mail and offer their comments on all manner of city business to Postmaster Bob Swearingen. This was evident when we asked Bob about the compact, lime-green building next door. Or, as it was known in Princeton: City Hall. One day each month, it opened so the mayor and four councilmen could conduct town business and hear citizen complaints. Bob volunteered that he "heard these complaints every day."

There was no eatery in the town, so we improvised. We planned to return the following morning with donuts; Bob offered coffee. We left

by Prince Street and drove past "Powell's Critter Haven Manor * * * Happy Hoppers Rabbitry." The only critters in residence this day were chickens.

The library in neighboring Richmond provided some history. A volunteer there actually grew up in Princeton. She also recalled researching all Princetons in school, but could not remember the number she found. Her grandfather was born in Princeton, Illinois, and died in Princeton, Kansas. Perhaps he followed Horace Greeley's advice to "Go west, young man!"

We inquired about notable events in Princeton. She quickly mentioned a murder but was hazy on details. Ten years ago? No, possibly 20 years ago. Over a woman? Or drugs? Maybe the guilty man was still in jail.

At lunch in a nearby town, we met realtor Don Poss and told him we had driven past an ostrich farm. It turns out there was also an emu farm and a buffalo farm nearby. Emus, he understood, were less contrary than ostriches and much tastier. "Did you know the healing powers of emu oil?" he asked. The stuff was reported to have amazing properties. A woman he knew had long-suffered from arthritis. She started rubbing the afflicted areas with emu oil and completely eliminated the pain in 14 months.

Back at the Princeton Post Office the following morning, Bob was waiting for us. We avoided any health code violations by eating breakfast outside. The weather was cold but bearable. Donuts and Bob's hot coffee on the hood of our Buick met our "Breakfast in Princeton" criteria.

Bob was a 20-year Navy man and was content to be a small town postmaster. He restored antique cars. His wife, a nurse, was into crafts. One of their sons wanted to get out of the small town, got a good job in Chicago, hated it, moved back and bought 40 acres of land nearby.

With our cards postmarked we headed home after a brief stop at *The Ottawa Herald*. What major news events had occurred in the past year, we wondered. The one they could recall was the annual "Princeton City Wide Yard Sale" in early May.

Three Princetons were now behind us. Each was unique and had provided us with unexpected encounters.

TRIP #2

Indiana
Kentucky

"Sorry, no gravy this morning."

...waitress at Emma Lou's Sandwich Shop

Princeton, Indiana
Population: 8,127
Breakfast for two: $8.19 plus tip

The December 1 *Daily Clarion* banner headline proclaimed "TOYOTA COMES TO PRINCETON." Several months later on Valentine's Day, the *Clarion* covered our visit, although it didn't have the same economic impact as the new Toyota plant.

Town center had a distinctive old-town ambiance. Notable buildings included the Classical Revival railroad depot (circa 1895), the Art Deco theatre (circa 1920) with four screens and seats at $1.75, and the Beaux Arts Post Office (circa 1911).

At the center of town was the stately Romanesque Revival style Gibson County Court House (circa 1884). It was a bright red brick building with black walnut and oak interior and mosaic tile floors. The cornerstone listed among its inventory "one set of artificial teeth."

The Court House was the site of a landmark case. In 1955 a "gentlemanly" young construction worker accused of six "mad dog" murders was tried for one of them. The accused was said to have left 30 cents with each victim. The designation "30" has long been used as newspaper code for "end of the story." A guilty verdict was appealed all the way to

the Supreme Court. It was overturned on grounds that local publicity denied the defendant a fair trial. A retrial found him guilty and he received a life sentence.

Four years earlier, a Mrs. Clarence Spurlock was tried there for murdering her parents by feeding them arsenic. She was found not guilty. Perhaps her husband should have watched more closely when she prepared his dinner since "large amounts" of arsenic were reportedly found in his body when he died.

Notable Princetonians included Orville Redenbacher, who got his start as a manager at Princeton Farms. Not surprisingly, the facility was renowned for its popcorn. Dodger great Gil Hodges lived in Princeton as a child.

The Gil Hodges Baseball Field bore his name and was home of the American Legion Post #25 Tigers.

Dick Clark's Restaurant was the popular dinner choice. It had no relationship to the "American Bandstand" host. Richard Clark was a World War II vet who figured out in 1946 that ice cream would be all the rage, so he bought a Taylor ice cream freezer and 12 cans for $2,479, and began churning out quality ice cream. In busy summer months, Clark's hires as many as 47 carhops. We asked our waitress, a high school senior, what she did for fun. She replied, "Go cruising and go to the movies." Cruising is exactly what we did, heading back to our motel.

Breakfast was an obvious choice: Emma Lou's Sandwich Shop on the square. It had only a neon sign saying "CAFE - Air Conditioned." One early morning last April, someone tossed a rock through the front window. The glass was replaced but no one had bothered to repaint the name.

Kyla Jo Wethington greeted us and promptly informed us, "Sorry, no gravy this morning." Kyla was a third generation waitress at Emma Lou's. She was fretting about a planned drive to New Orleans that afternoon with her boyfriend for Mardi Gras. Her expectations were sky high; her anxiety up there too, perhaps because she had no reservations. There was also the matter of her balky car. Kyla Jo considered using

her father's Lincoln. If it broke down, she could call him to come pick them up.

The passion for Indiana basketball and the color red was evident at Emma Lou's. Red and white Hoosier posters and schedules filled the wall. Another proclaimed Indiana as the Big Red State. Indiana's infamous coach Bobby Knight was considered "competitive," not the bully some media reports suggested.

The *Daily Clarion*'s Sue Ellen Parker learned of our presence from patrons of the restaurant the night before. She covered our visit and appropriately had the principal and us photographed with the life-sized tiger statue at the Princeton Community High School entrance.

A must stop at "Greeks" for hand-dipped chocolate, a cup of coffee from Kyla, and we were off to Kentucky.

"No, that's wasteful. Just two."

.... local feed storeowner

Princeton, Kentucky
Population: 6,940
Breakfast for two: $6.83 plus tip

The town owed its name to an early settler named William Prince. It originally was called Prince's Place. It was the Caldwell County seat and definitely Bible Belt country. The county was dry.

At first glance, the town seemed a bit forlorn, bypassed by the Interstate Highway System and destined to stagnate. In fact, many of its original buildings had found new uses. At West Court Square an intriguing Victorian brick building featured ornate medallions with terra cotta busts over bay windows. It was originally a Masonic Lodge (1899), then a post office. On our visit it housed "Princeton 1-Hour Cleaners."

Princeton was once known as the "Athens of the Pennyrile" for its educational institutions. In 1873, young ladies boarded at the college for $80 for a 20-week term. Young gentlemen had to live elsewhere. Curious about the name "Pennyrile," we visited the library where we found that "Pennyrile" was really a plant named "Penny Royal."

Another plant played a greater part in the area's history. Tobacco. The region produced much of the world's supply of dark tobacco, the basis for chewing tobacco. The annual Black Patch Festival celebrated the harvest. This year no one coveted the Miss Black Patch title so the incumbent was asked to reign again.

Tobacco had a long and often violent history here. The Black Patch Tobacco War was considered "the largest civil uprising in the United States between the Civil War and the 1960s race riots." In the early 1900s, the American Tobacco Company fixed prices below cost and farmers rebelled, organizing the "Night Riders." The 5,000 riders burned warehouses and even whipped those friendly with the company. In 1911, the U.S. Supreme Court upheld an order breaking

up American Tobacco's monopoly. The local doctor who led the Riders was acquitted of wrongdoing.

We stopped by Newsom's Old Mill Store (established in 1917). It occupied a mill built in 1850. The adjoining building was a tavern and hotel built in 1840 and now used for storage. Colonel Bill Newsom, the store owner, told us it had been a good arrangement since patrons who overdid libations in the tavern were carried upstairs to hotel rooms, no doubt being charged for lodging during their recovery.

Newsom's was known for its country-smoked hams, thanks in part to a 1975 story by the chef and author James Beard. Other national publications including *The Wine Spectator*, *Food & Wine* and *Women's Day* followed suit and recommended the colonel's ham.

Nancy, the colonel's daughter, known around town as "the ham lady," enthusiastically explained the aging process. In August the hams were ready for Christmas, though some aficionados preferred hams that had a few months more aging. Nancy would only say that yearly output was in the low thousands.

Buckets of seeds were available, so I couldn't resist snow peas, onion sets and potatoes for my small backyard garden. Colonel Bill recommended the Kennebec (Maine) seed potatoes. I wanted to confirm that I'd need three eyes in each slice planted, but the colonel said, "No, that's wasteful. Just two."

Breakfast was at Poe's Cafe, once a grocery store. Its nine tables filled an ample open area with a counter in the rear. The walls were sparsely decorated. The customers were mostly men clad in jackets, plaid shirts, jeans, laced boots. They all wore baseball caps with logos of Chevron, Lone Star Feed-Fertilizer, and Rollison Logging Equipment.

Our waitress greeted us with a "howdy" and hot coffee. It took the chill off a surprise early morning snowfall. I asked about pancakes and the waitress cautioned that they were big. She thought it unlikely I could eat the three-stack listed in the menu so I ordered two at 85 cents each, sausage patties and milk. Garie had #3, a scrambled egg, sausage patty and a pancake.

After our now-customary stop at the post office to postmark cards and fuel for our Buick Century, Princeton number five was behind us.

TRIP #3

Arkansas
Louisana
Texas

"Stories and lies"
...95-year old, lifetime resident

Princeton, Arkansas
Population: 50
Breakfast for two: $6.03

W e headed south from St. Louis to Arkansas on St. Patrick's Day. A cold rain greeted our arrival in Princeton. Our first stop was the J-Mart Food Store in the heart of town. Signs advertised COLD BEER and FINA gas. A white canopy sheltered the two gas pumps and shaded a long wooden bench where, in warmer days, old timers sat for hours.

The warm reception helped us forget the dreariness outside. Bernice Nelson opened the store at 6 a.m. and worked behind the counter. George Matthews sat on a stack of beer cases. Within minutes we too became part of the scene as Bernice delighted in telling customers about our odyssey.

The store carried all manner of goods, ranging from hunting caps and shot gun shells to soft drinks and a wide selection of beer. A menu listed sausage/egg rolls for 99 cents. That would be our breakfast the next morning.

Inquiries at the county seat led us to Judge Troy Bradley, a 1957 graduate of Princeton High School. The sports teams in Judge Bradley's day were known as the Princeton Hornets. In 1965, after consolidating with Fordyce High, they unhappily became the Fordyce Redbugs. The redbug is a small insect found in pine forests. It finds the trees unappetizing, but feasts happily on humans, inflicting painful bites. Thankfully, we encountered neither hornets nor redbugs.

Timber was the sole industry but hunting helped the economy. Bernice tagged more than 1,000 deer the previous fall. "Were there many accidents?" we asked. "Not as many as you'd think," Bernice said, "but one man got hurt twice." The unlucky hunter shot himself in the hand climbing over a fence. Three years later, he broke a hip falling out of a tree stand. Ending the story Bernice added, "Come to think of it, he was 80. Maybe shouldn't have been climbing tree stands."

The oldest resident was Henry Foote "Foots" Coleman, born October 24, 1900. He was a lifelong Princetonian and an original stockholder in the Fordyce Bank and Trust Company. We asked if he knew any stories about Princeton. He replied, "Yeah, stories and lies." Foots had once been in St. Louis, in 1930 to see the World Series between the Cardinals and Philadelphia.

Mr. Coleman, as he is called by most, recalled a story (not a lie) from his youth. Seemed his father and the sheriff were bringing food to

the jail. They unlocked the door and found not only the six prisoners but also young (Mr.) Coleman. "How did you get in here?" father asked. "Shinnied through the bars," he answered. "I was small then."

Anticipating our arrival in the morning, Bernice made several batches of sausage/egg biscuits. Nolin Steelman, 77, bantered with her while he waited for the mail. Nolin offered to show us the cemetery. En route we passed, of all things, a primitive golf course in the pine forest. A sign on the pillars at the cemetery entrance read: "Before excavation please call either Elmer Smith, Nora Smith or Lorice Rogers." It listed their phone numbers and the message, "Peace and rest to the weary."

The cemetery was established in 1845. A chain link fence separated the white and black burial plots. There was one headstone, Edwin Eugene Harris, a surgeon in Clarke's Brigade. Without headstones, the other Civil War casualties buried here remain unknown.

At the Senior Center, two cooks gave us a tutorial in sorting spoiled and hard bits from black-eyed peas. We accepted their invitation for lunch the next day, where we enjoyed ham, black-eyed peas, cabbage, sweet potatoes and Kool-Aid with many of our J-Mart acquaintances. The conversation was local in flavor: the town's past, the need for more rain, and Mr. Coleman's upcoming cataract surgery.

The J-Mart proved to be both our first stop and our last. With good-byes and complimentary coffee, we headed to Louisiana.

"Princeton
is a pretty name."

...Dolly McCade Prince, who named the town

Princeton, Louisiana
Population: 250
Breakfast for two (and postmaster): $4.70

W e followed the sign to Princeton on State Route 157, but this Princeton proved elusive. We passed a refinery and were certain the town center would quickly appear. There was nothing. We retraced our steps, looking for something—anything—a general store, post office, perhaps a cafe. The only sign of a town was a Baptist church, neat bungalows, mobile homes and the Princeton Middle School.

Temporarily defeated, we asked directions from a woman outside her home. We arrived at the post office as Postmaster Cline Henry, Jr. was closing up shop. Yes, there was a Princeton, Louisana. It's a blip on the map in Bossier

Parish. The original town center was near the church. The general store had succumbed to a fire five years ago.

In 1909, Dolly McCade Prince, the wife of a plantation owner, was asked to name the town. "McCade" was already used in Louisiana. So was her next choice, "Princeville." Mrs. Prince went with a variation and declared, "Princeton is a pretty name."

The cotton and sugar cane fields were long gone, the old saw mill a distant memory. A local retiree described the town as "just a bunch of houses." We found a bit more: three churches and F-S Prestress, a company that made concrete precasts for bridges and parking garages. The F-S building, at two stories, was the tallest structure in town. Yes, it had a pre-cast facade.

We saw T's Station and Cafe near the post office. Could this be our Princeton breakfast? Geographically, it didn't qualify. Cline said the cafe's mailbox was moved from Mahaffey Road on the western border of town, over to Highway 80. Technically, it was in nearby Hutton. Plan B: Donuts and coffee with the postmaster after he finished sorting mail.

We asked the Bossier City branch library staff if there had been any excitement in recent times. One librarian said there had been some near-murders. She wanted to "kill" her husband a couple of times.

In 1913, a Bossier County resident received a patent for the ingenious red flag on rural mailboxes that tells the postman there's outgoing mail. In 1934 Bonnie and Clyde passed through. In 1973, a little girl supposedly found a diamond in her gravel driveway. The Diamond Trade Company was formed and the gravel company, the presumed source, fenced in its gravel pits. Then the truth came out. The diamond was from Arkansas and not even gem quality.

While enjoying donuts and coffee with Cline outside the post office, we asked a customer to take our photo. He was Mark Norris, a canoe outfitter, who invited us to see the largest cedar canoe in Louisiana. It was made in New Mexico of western cedar, was 37 feet long and weighed 450 pounds. It carried 18 people and over 3,500 pounds. Norris bought

it for $15,000 and offered gourmet dinner floats in nearby bayous along-side 400-year-old cypress.

Clifton "Clif" Cardin, "Official Bossier Parish Historian," provided a couple of intriguing stories involving folks who shared our surname. One (circa 1908) was the tale of teachers Lucy Perry and John Carstar-phen, reportedly courting on school time. Carstarphen accused another teacher of instigating the trouble, insulted her publicly and said he had dirt on the principal. Carstarphen was not suspended. Most of the teachers walked out. The school board president fired the principal. Clif didn't mention whether John and Lucy lived happily ever after.

The second (circa 1921) involved James Perry, a cashier at the

Plain Dealing Bank. A bank audit revealed false entries in the ledgers. The bank had been insolvent for five years. Perry admitted the false entries, but claimed he didn't take the missing $121,000. We do know what happened to James. Ten years in prison.

Our unlikely blood relationship to either of the infamous Perrys had not raised an eyebrow during our visit, so we thought it prudent to head for Texas before sundown. And so we did.

"... or two evenings if they go to church regularly."

...one of nine rules for teachers in 1872

Princeton, Texas
Population: 2,321
Breakfast for two: $4.57

The post office was closed when we arrived so we found the police station. There we met Officers O'Day and Cantrell. When Officer Cantrell heard of our venture he graciously produced a town map and excused himself. Within minutes he returned with a woman whom he said was just the person we should meet.

She was Helen Lawson, school tax collector and councilperson. We accepted her invitation to stop by her office the next morning. She promised us a copy of *Princeton, Area History and Little Known "Facts."*

Helen and the officers recommended Rader's

Restaurant for dinner, and breakfast at The Sweet Shop. The other option for breakfast was Dairy Queen but they felt it lacked small town ambiance.

The Sweet Shop it was. Wilma Alderson was behind the counter. This was really a donut shop with a bit more. Every morning the shop sold about 200 biscuits filled with sausage or with eggs and sausage. We got the

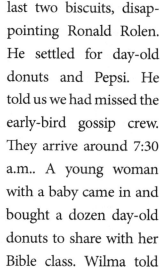

last two biscuits, disappointing Ronald Rolen. He settled for day-old donuts and Pepsi. He told us we had missed the early-bird gossip crew. They arrive around 7:30 a.m.. A young woman with a baby came in and bought a dozen day-old donuts to share with her Bible class. Wilma told us donuts were marked down to a dollar a dozen after noon. Marty, the milk deliveryman who stopped by, admitted he didn't drink milk.

Wilma's son, who owned the shop, also took special orders. The night before, he and an associate had made 50 dozen-sausage biscuits plus 20 dozen glazed donuts for kids who were at the Collin County Model Farm for their annual exhibition.

This Princeton, like many others, traced its roots to the railroad. It is situated on a land grant dating back to 1844. At that time, "there were two groups of Indians living in the area—friendly and unfriendly." Disputes over mixed-up land grants disturbed the peace as much as constant Indian fights. Settlers hoping for more often sold their land for 25 to 50 cents an acre and returned to their former homes. By 1870, cotton displaced corn as the major crop. It remained so today in the black, nutrient-rich soil.

Onions were of no consequence now, but Princeton pioneered onion production in North Texas, as early as 1906. Back then, a yellow onion known as the "Prize-Taker" report-edly tasted as "hot as a firecracker." It soon gave way to milder varieties. Bermuda onions were introduced in 1923. A record yield of 297 railcars and many truckloads were shipped in 1936. An article in 1938 closed as follows, "Princeton has always been partial to local labor in setting out and harvesting its crop, at no time calling in foreign labor from the South Texas area."

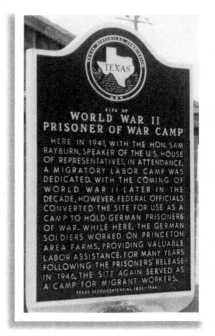

Economics soon changed this modus operandi. In 1940 a labor

camp was built for up to 400 migrants who worked during the onion and cotton seasons. The late Sam Rayburn, Speaker of the U.S. House of Representatives, dedicated the camp in 1941. It served as a German prisoner of war camp for eight months in 1945. We learned that some farmers and prisoners corresponded for many years. The camp closed years later and was now a recreation park.

Years ago these Texas teachers must have needed rules. So did the educators in Princeton, Louisiana, but that's another story. Among the nine rules set forth in 1872 were:

> **-Men teachers may take one evening each week for courting purposes, or two evenings if they go to church regularly.**
>
> **-Woman teachers who marry or engage in unseemly conduct will be dismissed.**
>
> **-The teacher who performs his labor faithfully and without fault for five years will be given an increase of twenty-five cents per week, providing the Board of Education approves.**

No wonder teachers eventually unionized.

TRIP #4

California, San Mateo County
California, Colusa County
Oregon
Idaho

"OOO-ga! OOO-ga!"

...imitation of a ship's horn

Princeton (By-The-Sea), California (San Mateo County)
Population: 150
Breakfast for two: $18.35 plus tip

We decided early on that Princeton-By-The-Sea, despite its hyphenated name, qualified as a breakfast destination. At lunch en route, Lee Murphy, a Hertz Car Manager, overheard us and said he lived in Princeton. Like most locals, he omitted the words "By-The-Sea." He said they did eat breakfast by the sea—at Ketch-Joanne's.

In 1908, Frank P. Brophy, owner of beach properties along the Ocean Shore Railroad, planned to make the town into the "Coney Island of the Pacific." He envisioned thousands of people taking the 45-minute rail trip south from San Francisco.

The railroad folded in 1922, as did Brophy's plans. Prohibition pumped new life into the area in the form of rum. The Princeton Inn drew San Francisco clientele who wanted to drink "safely" away from home. Some tipplers risked driving their expensive Pierce Arrows on the dangerous San Pedro Mountain Road to reach this and other "safe havens" around Half Moon Bay. The Princeton Inn did not escape notice. It was raided and repeatedly closed for breaking the Red Light Abatement Act, suggesting that more than booze was available.

We cruised the streets and found Princeton, Harvard, Yale, Stanford, West Point, and Columbia Avenues. Vassar Street didn't achieve avenue status, likely because it was only a two-block, gravel alley.

The town was eclectic: a tourist hotel, restaurants, condos, prefabbed warehouses, lots heaped with crab traps, boat repair yards, small homes, some with ancient boats alongside, and huge eucalyptus trees.

The sea was the basis of the economy, though not how Brophy expected. Salmon, rockfish, tuna, crab and squid were commercially caught. Whale watching excursions ran from December to March.

Garie introduced herself to several men outside American Legion Post 474. Richard Moran was a merchant seaman and the only local we met who called the town "Princeton-By-The-Sea." Roy Rosin remembered when there were two canneries in town (shades of Steinbeck) and

artichoke fields. He recalled Brussels sprouts replacing artichokes but lamented that recent sprouts "were not sweet like they used to be."

Everyone knew MacDonald Smith, a/k/a "Ooga." He had served in Vietnam and was a part owner of the Pemberton Fish Company. His nickname originated when inspectors couldn't find a horn on his boat and asked him about its absence. Smith assured them he had a horn, rushed to the side and bellowed "OOO-ga! OOOG-ga!" He replicated the horn for us, much to the delight of the bar patrons.

When we mentioned that we were heading north to the other Princeton, Ooga moaned. Several years ago Pemberton bought a $100,000 smoking oven in Oregon. A $60/hour crane awaited its delivery. One, two days passed and no oven arrived. Meanwhile, the crane sat idle with the meter running.

The oven appeared on day three. It turned out the driver saw a sign to Princeton on his way south. He figured he made good time and left the highway to rest. Unfortunately, it was the Princeton in Colusa County. The driver spent a restful night roadside, then realized his mistake when he couldn't find the processing plant. We learned Ooga's partner restrained him from tossing the driver into the oven. We avoided more

painful memories and didn't ask about the total crane cost.

Ketch-Joanne for breakfast. Several fishermen were having coffee in an alcove whose walls were covered with photographs of fishing boats. A

wood-burning stove warmed the room. Our waitress, Caroline, brought the special egg and salmon scramble. Talking with the men we soon learned of their fishing-related ailments, especially arthritis. Too bad we had no emu oil with us.

In Ooga's processing plant, our taste buds perked up as we watched salmon being sliced into thin, diagonal slices and packaged. Of course, we saw the misdirected oven. Ooga gave us a package of smoked salmon as a parting gift.

The salmon didn't make it far beyond the Bay Bridge as we travelled north to the other California Princeton.

45

"The paint was on sale."

...Princeton ferry captain

Princeton, California (Colusa County)
Population: 405
Breakfast for two: $11.66 plus tip

Our letter to the postmaster found its way to "professional volunteer" Mary Beth Massas. She volunteered at the library and was looking forward to showing us around the small farming community. If not for her and other volunteers, the library couldn't operate—it lost its county funding for paid employees some years earlier. Mary Beth was one of those caring people every small town seems to have. We were not surprised to find 39 of her recipes in *The Best of Princeton* cookbook she gave us.

Princeton was about 75 miles north-west of Sacramento. The area was flat but fertile. In 1858, a home-steader who

lived nearby observed, "There was to be seen between my place and Princeton but one house, if a box set upon the plain could be so designated." The flatness and available water were ideal for growing rice.

The Princeton Ferry operated 16 hours a day, carrying vehicles 500 feet across the Sacramento River. The 50-cent, three-minute ride saved locals 12 to 13 miles of driving. The ferry was built in 1950 from 30 Navy surplus pontoons. It was the fourth vessel to operate since 1858. We drove on board for the short round-trip voyage.

The ferry operator's card read "Cap-Tin" John (Harroun). He proudly explained how an 80-1 gear ratio transferred the power of the 3 horsepower motor to the cable drive that pulled the ferry from shore to shore. Why, we asked John, were the rice elevators on the south side of town painted an unlikely cream color? His explanation, "The paint was on sale."

California Route 45 led to and from the town, but in the town it morphed into the business district on Commercial Street. At the north end, a white sign painted with two fading American flags informed motorists that they were "Entering a Home Rule County."

We searched the archives of the town newspaper, *The Broadcaster*. In the November 18, 1929 issue, the stock market crash seemed of little importance. It reported in detail the local football team's 6-0 loss. The November 29 edition had better news: a season-ending 12-6 win. In the LOST & FOUND column was this item:

LOST: A fountain pen by a man half full of ink.

No reward

For breakfast, we headed to Gonzales'. Noelia Gonzales was the owner and cook. Noelia heard our knock and opened the door well before the posted starting hour. Mexican music and Noelia's chitchat echoed from the kitchen as we partook of a typical American breakfast of fried eggs (over easy, thank you), bacon, toast and coffee. The Mexican touches in the restaurant were Noelia's idea to attract some of the many Hispanics in the area.

At our early morning coffee at the library, Mary Beth suggested the

Princeton Market for a unique T-shirt. Owner Guy Gomes knew we were coming. He had owned the independent store for

five years, selling groceries, meat, beer, wine and liquor. He produced the T-shirt, which had a picture of a scruffy group of people and one "Daisy Mae type" working around a car. It posed the question, "WHERE THE HELL'S PRINCETON, CALIFORNIA?" Of course I bought one.

Our perfunctory photo in front of the post office took on new proportions when we were greeted by a group of warm-up-suited ladies whom we dubbed "The Ladies Walking Society of Princeton, California." They gladly joined the postmaster and us for the photo.

As we drove through the countryside, we realized how the land had blessed the area. We passed almond, plum and walnut orchards, and olive groves. Rich, brown rice paddies were waiting for the flooding and planting window. Fields of winter wheat were green. Trucks carrying sugar beets moved along the highway. And for our departure, pheasants and magpies appeared along the roadside to bid us bon voyage on the way to Oregon.

"I don't reach for anything now."

...Contract mail carrier

Princeton, Oregon
Population: 100
Breakfast for two and a mail carrier: $5.69

L ots of space, few people. That's Harney County where this Princeton was located. Space here was a relative term. Harney County's 10,185 square miles were larger than the combined area of Connecticut, Rhode Island and Delaware. But that vast space had a population of only 7,050, less than each of the Princetons we would visit in New Jersey, Indiana and Illinois.

At the Palace Cafe in Burns several men told us that despite the AAA map which only showed New Princeton, there was a real Princeton. When State Route 78 was re-routed, an ill-informed cartographer omitted it. Any eateries or other businesses were things of the past. Undaunted, we loaded

up with coffee and glazed doughnuts from a Safeway.

We found the Princeton Post Office, the smallest one we had visited. It was in a white shed just off a gravel road. Postmaster Mike Maaske was a wiry man in his forties with full beard. He was sweeping snow from walkways. The public area with access to the window and boxes was a compact four feet

square. Box rental was a bargain, $2 a year. Such a price tempted us to rent one just to have a Princeton, Oregon, address.

The post office sign was the original one, dating back to 1910. In the late 1920s the post office was in the home of Barney and Edith Graft Kobler. Edith was the postmaster. The Koblers got into an argument with Banty Nelson, a stagecoach driver. Banty shot and killed Barney and Edith quit as postmaster.

When contract mail carrier Diane Priest arrived we had a guest for breakfast

and a dining table of sorts, her truck hood. Diane covered a 150-mile route, and had just recovered from recent injury, a crushed pelvis. Her truck rolled over when she lost control reaching for a letter. She said, "I don't reach for anything now!" as she reached for a doughnut.

At least one person picked up his own mail. A rancher who managed nearly a half-million acres flew to the post office. He landed his plane on the county road, walked to the post office, picked up his mail, and returned for takeoff.

Mike pointed out "New" Princeton. To the northwest, a building with two residents. To the east, a distant ranch where the third resident lived. A solitary llama watched from a fenced area as we looked over the site of the old Princeton center. The surviving "town" was a few abandoned shacks. No sign of the old school.

The few children who lived in Princeton attended school in Crane. Parents drove younger children up to 30 miles for class. Some Crane High school students came from neighboring Nevada about 100 miles away. These and others who didn't commute lived in school dormitories.

The Harney Electric Cooperative brought power to Princeton in 1957 and changed dry-land ranches to irrigated fields. Farmers grew oats, wheat, alfalfa and hay during the short season. Less hardy crops would be vulnerable to frost which was possible any month. Bales of hay provided food and shelter for herds of Black Angus and Hereford.

We saw bullet holes in the route signs and figured they were expressions of local independence. Rancher Jim Ausmus told us the vegetation blowing across the road was sagebrush, rabbit brush and greasewood.

Leaving town, we realized this Princeton had no discernible boundaries. The vastness of the ranges and the shadows of the buttes had swallowed up what had been a town. Schools and the nearest tavern were in Crane. Commerce was handled in Burns. The high desert country offered isolation. The people who lived on the ranches and in solitary mobile homes marched to the beat of their own drummers. Perhaps that's what the eastern homesteader sought when he came west and founded the town in 1910.

"You'll have a proper breakfast here."

...Postmaster, Princeton, Idaho

Princeton, Idaho
Population: 75
Breakfast for two: Courtesy of Postmaster Glenda Germen

The town was literally a wide part of State Route 6. Most of the homes, some mobile, were on the north side. Town life revolved around the GasMart, Princeton Tavern and the post office. May's 2nd Hand & Antiques, the Grange and a grain elevator got little play.

Postmaster Glenda Germen was expecting us. It was easy to picture

this former one-story general store with hitching posts for horses and wagons where pick-up trucks now parked. We spotted a small window inside, about a foot square, directly below the main window. Glenda's predecessor made it for his dog. Now Glenda handled mail through it to small tots who came with their parents. Had we found the lowest working window in the U. S. Postal Service?

For 14 years, Glenda had been postmaster. That's post-MASTER, she emphasized. The postal service has no postmistress title. Glenda was painfully shy early in her career. Rather than ask a customer for a few cents for returned mail, she'd make it up with spare change from her pocket. One day she decided shyness must go. We found it hard to believe that this effervescent postmaster had ever been shy.

Eric Kurtz stopped by for his mail. He came from near St. Louis and knew where we lived. He and his wife had travelled through the area, liked it, sold the family concrete business and moved here. He designed their energy-efficient underground concrete house. Skylights illuminated the interior and a mere four cords of wood heated it all winter. He raised hay and helped his wife who bred registered Salers and Simmentals. Recently she transferred 32 quality embryos to surrogate cows.

We offered to bring donuts and coffee the next morning for our protocol breakfast. "Absolutely no!" Glenda said, "You'll have a proper breakfast here."

Glenda told us she listened to the troubles of people who don't drink. Al at the Princeton Tavern listened to those who do drink. We had no troubles but a beer with Al seemed like a good idea

The first "B" at the Rolling Hills Bed & Breakfast renewed us, but we passed up the second "B" for Glenda's invitation. Sizzling bacon, coffee and fresh orange juice greeted our arrival. Glenda and her 12-year old daughter, Katie, were preparing breakfast. Potatoes were being "hash-browned" in an electric skillet, followed by eggs over-lightly. Toast came courtesy of bread made by Glenda's 84-year old father. It was indeed a "proper" breakfast served

on the sorting table. Glenda forgot to raise the flag until well into the meal. We hope that was the only regulation broken.

Before leaving, we fueled up at the GasMart. On the counter was a dish of cigarettes at 15 cents each. Crystal Mantz, the clerk, explained that these were for people giving up smoking so the remainder of a full pack would not tempt them. Among the 18 varieties of hunting and fishing licenses for sale: a lifetime pass for a one-year-old for $501.50. Two-year-olds

(and up to 50) paid $701.50. Wait until 51 and pay only $401.50.

Crystal recalled the time she overfilled a tank, gushing gas all over the ground. The customer was an environmentalist who insisted she clean it up thoroughly. It took an hour. Crystal still lamented that the customer wasn't a local farmer who simply would have said it was just like his driveway.

In the back of the store was a beauty parlor and a welding shop, probably not used for unwieldy hair. Cathy Nowack—proprietress of the Cuts 'n' Curls beauty parlor—moved here when she married a local man. Crystal was quick to point out that local men *only* marry outsiders. They can't risk marrying the local girls since everyone knew too much about them. "I knew her when…" might threaten the marriage.

We had a thought as we left. If the Postmaster General seriously wanted to improve customer satisfaction, all employees should emulate Glenda Germen.

TRIP #5

Ohio
Pennsylvania
New York

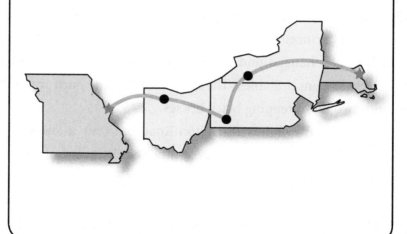

"And cats!"

...lifetime resident

Princeton, Ohio
Population: 150
Breakfast for two: $0.00 (Coffee and donuts from motel)

The town seemed to start off well in 1816 with a post office and shortly after, a tavern. Then came tanning, carding and pork-packing plants. "Wisky [*sic*] was also a large product." History recorded that "Princeton was a lively business center in early times."

Things had changed and not for the better. The last commercial enterprise was Sunset Stables. The now-vacant white barn was silhouetted with two high stepping black horses.

People seemed to know Princeton Road but only a few knew the existence of Princeton itself. The post office clerks heard of the routes that served Princeton Road but not of the town of 150 on a road map.

We drove to the Indian Springs town administration complex since the county sheriff's office indicated Princeton was in Indian Springs' jurisdiction. Not so, said the Indian Springs police, it's under the sheriff's jurisdiction, we're just the back-up. We felt for Princeton, now an orphan after such a robust start.

Two Indian Springs fireman actually knew where the town was so we asked them, "Anything exciting happen in Princeton lately?" One recalled that several years ago a woman and her boyfriend claimed the woman's husband had committed suicide by shooting himself with a crossbow. Their story didn't fly. He was shot with *two* arrows and the defense couldn't produce a "double-barreled" crossbow.

The town was a cluster of homes and several farms around the intersection of Princeton-Glendale Road and Princeton Road. The intersection was on a modest hill. The town extended less than a mile in each

direction. Two water towers loomed over the tree line. Both were emblazoned with the words "Butler County."

The water towers were the backdrop to our breakfast at the intersection. Vehicles stopping and starting at the traffic light provided sound and light. Coffee and donuts completed our outdoor breakfast theatre.

There were no signs of life around town, except one man mowing his lawn. The narrow road and traffic behind prevented us from stopping to ask him about the area. Too bad we couldn't communicate with the numerous dogs we saw.

Early New Jersey settlers may have given the town its name. They had named a nearby town for New Jersey's capital, Trenton. Other area town names—Maud, Excello, Overpeck, Seven Mile, Blue Ball and Red Lion—shed no light on the naming.

We had yet to talk to a resident when we visited our last planned stop, the *Journal-News* in Hamilton. None of the news staff was from Princeton nor did they know anyone from the town. So we departed for Pennsylvania via Princeton, hopeful of meeting a resident.

Success! Driving back we noticed a woman by her mailbox. As we stopped she hesitated, then waved and came over to greet us. She was Mary Arnold, born 70 years ago on a farm just below the hill. Her

husband Vern joined us. He actually saw us earlier in the day when we stopped to take a picture of Wynds of Liberty, a subdivision taking shape on former farmland. Vern speculated from seeing my awkward stance to frame the subdivision with a tree that I was a birdwatcher, focusing on a rare species.

Vern was also born in Princeton. He had known Mary from childhood. They moved here a year ago from the east side where they had lived in an "antique" home which they had painstakingly restored over 32 years. Now they were in a more manageable home and had more time for their "pontoon" on a Kentucky Lake.

We told them we were surprised by seeing only one man yesterday, a schoolboy this morning and now Mary. Vern explained that people were all working and agreed that everyone had dogs. He added, "And cats!" As for natives, they knew of only two others, a farmer in his seventies and a lady in her nineties.

"Doesn't that jar your applesauce!"
-Norma "Skinny" Gibson

Princeton, Pennsylvania
Population: 150
Breakfast for two: Courtesy of Bill Dean, "Mayor" of Princeton

Had we not seen Scott Kaminsky and his two dogs in his front lawn, we might have driven until nightfall without finding Princeton. The map was inexact about its location and our blind reckoning non-productive. Scott quieted his dogs and came over. Yes, this could be considered Princeton, but the village was along the road we had turned off. "You will see a 'Village of Princeton' sign."

The village extended less than half a mile on a hill where two roads merged at the Princeton Memorial Presbyterian Church (1870). The merger became the main street lined by frame homes, some offset by a few feet.

Our motel for the night required

an agreement that we take our pets out if they barked. Our pets were two cats, so we signed with impunity.

Seeing no eateries or commerce in Princeton, we brought coffee and donuts to the church parking area for our breakfast. When Garie thought of another donut, she added a raisin English muffin from the motel.

Ed Harlan came across the street to greet us. He was a dairy

farmer with a herd of 39 cows. He declined coffee and donut, but offered to introduce us to his neighbor, "Skinny" Gibson, who "knew as much about the town as anyone."

We weren't comfortable addressing an 85-year old lady as "Skinny," "Mrs. Gibson" seemed more appropriate. She was born in Princeton and her parents owned a general store. She was the fourth of nine (or ten) children. She was unsure of the exact count. Her father gave each a nickname and Mrs. Gibson was a slightly built child. Her nearest sister was "Fuzzy," which described her hair.

Skinny remembered the post office, Kildoo's store and its candy, and the blacksmith shop. Ed told us his home was once a store but Skinny expressed doubt and planned "to get on Eddie about that." One of her childhood memories was learning how to plug in the lines at the telephone office.

Skinny's dog Snoops was wary of men so sat either under her or Garie's chair. Skinny proudly showed pictures of her children, who

had moved away and raised their own families. After realizing she misplaced a daughter's address, she e x c l a i m e d, "Doesn't that jar your apple-sauce!"

Judy Shaffer who "looked after" the church, recommended a favorite of locals, the b&b Charcoal Grill, for breakfast. We were unaware of b&b's specialty until we had finished a full breakfast. They offered at least 30 varieties of pie. Whole pies were available on one-day notice, more daring combinations of filling upon request. We could only manage sharing a slice of Dutch apple.

When we sat at the counter beside Bill Dean, our waitress, Donna, introduced him as her neighbor and "mayor" of Princeton. He was a

well driller and owned some old buildings in Princeton that he was renovating or tearing

down. When time came to pay, I noticed that Bill had slipped our check under his plate. I tried to retrieve it, to no avail. "Compliments of Princeton," he said.

At the *New Castle News* the latest from Princeton was an interview with Eva Mershimer, then 99. She remembered casting her first vote in 1920 and taking her one-year-old baby to the polls by horse and buggy. She was proud of a certificate for voting in 50 consecutive elections. "We have the privilege, we should take it," she said. "We (women) made a big fuss before when we couldn't."

After we were interviewed, we met newsroom staffer Carol. Her reaction to our sharing one piece of pie at b&b was swift: "One piece? Go back and get raspberry crumb *and* coconut meringue or banana cream."

En route to New York, we took Carol's advice and detoured to the b&b for two slices of pie to go, but we stuck with Dutch Apple.

"I don't make enough to be a mistress."
...Duanesburg postmaster

Princeto(w)n, New York
Population: 2,031
Breakfast for two: $2.59

John Milton wrote, "To err is human." He should have added, "but sometimes embarrassing." We drove by three signs pointing to the town and passed the sign on the red brick town hall before we were inside talking with Kathy Nilson and realized that she was clearly saying "Princetown." We were *not* in Princeton, New York. We were in Princetown. Even our cats, Frostie and Bai Tao, good spellers who accompanied us, didn't notice the superfluous "W."

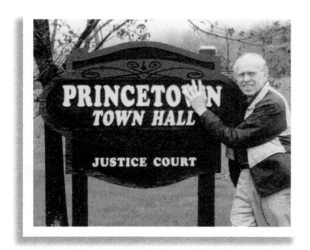

Several Princetons had originally been called Princetown. Within a few years of their founding, the name was contracted to Princeton. Logic would suggest this would occur in Princetown, New York. Early settlers were Scottish and

known for their pursuit of economy. One could assume they'd consider an unnecessary letter in their town's name an extravagance.

We told Irma Mastrean, who had authored *Princetown, Portrait of a Town*, about our odyssey and distress that her hometown's name did not conform to our spelling criterion. "Well", she said, "the newspapers often drop the 'w' when citing a person's residence in their

obituary." Thus some people lived in Princetown and died in Princeton. We henceforth referred to this town as Princeto(w)n in deference to the departed.

Princeto(w)n was described as "hilly and knolly" by an early settler. It was named for John Prince, a state assemblyman and local merchant. Perhaps not a good merchant since his last business failed. Irma's history recorded that

upon Prince's passing in 1801, "his debtors retained his body for sometime." History didn't reveal whether they got more than a pound of flesh from this strategy.

The nearest place to eat was the Duanesburg Diner, so we brought coffee and donuts to the town hall. (Our sixth makeshift breakfast so far.) We asked a state patrolman to take our picture. He kindly did, then asked where we came from. "St. Louis, Missouri," we answered. He surprised us by saying he was a Cardinal fan and showed us his identification badge. He was State Trooper Cardinal.

Today's town belied its heritage. The four discrete hamlets with stores, blacksmiths and churches that served the farming area at the turn of the century were gone. The Delaware and Hudson Railroad tracks seemed little used. The remaining focal points of community life were the town hall near one of the hamlets, Princetown Center, and two churches. Two working farms, some service-type businesses, a concrete operation, a pool company, water driller and a not-for-profit state center for the developmentally disabled were now the economic base for a town of rural living. Most residents worked elsewhere.

Except for two golf courses, there was little to attract outsiders, but the town judge had frequent "visitors" from throughout the country. These were the speeders who were stopped by the State Patrol along the six-mile stretch of I-88, which falls within the Princeto(w)n jurisdiction. Not a speed trap, mind you, but a windfall for a town that was in the right place when the interstate was built.

A legal notice on the town office bulletin board publicized a hearing to repeal an existing law, "Establishing Standards for Control of Pets in Princetown." The plan was to replace it with, "A Local Law for the Control of Activities of Dogs within the Town of Princetown." In days of big government, it was reassuring to know a dog's activities were still of local concern.

At the Duanesburg Post Office, Postmaster Barbara Thornton hand-cancelled our cards. When we commented about her title, she replied in jest, "Yes, I'm a postmaster. I don't make enough to be a mistress."

TRIP #6

Massachusetts

"from the seventh great-granddaughter of Princeton's first postmaster"

...the postmaster

Princeton, Massachusetts
Population: 3,189
Breakfast for two: $10.01 plus tip

The road we took into Princeton, Massachusetts, was arched with trees and bordered by stonewalls. We looked forward to New England ambience and heritage. We certainly wouldn't be disappointed.

It was a fitting entrance for a town that was settled in 1739, had 19 pre-Revolutionary homes and no gas stations. Remarkably, one family had lived on a family farm for ten generations.

There were seven graveyards, or burying grounds, in town. We stopped by the oldest on Mountain Road. It was in a hollow enclosed by a stone fence and sheltered by stately trees. The late afternoon sun cast slanting shadows across the slate markers. American flags honored Sons of the Revolution. Surely some were at Breed's Hill and waited until they saw the whites of British eyes.

A three-member Board of Selectmen governed the town. Among their duties was appointing an "Inspector of Wires," "Tree Warden and Moth Superintendent" and "Surveyor of Wood, Bark, Board, Shingles and Clapboards."

Princeton's earliest economy was agricultural. Light manufacturing followed in the 1800s, only to lose out to "summer people" who were attracted to the beauty of the town's elevated location (1,182 feet) and nearby Wachusett Mountain and Lake. In the late 1800s it boasted of 13 hotels. Their long porches were lined with rocking chairs. Some regular guests who stayed all summer brought their own rockers. In 1900, five trains passed through the town daily. The hotels and trains were gone now.

A 1900 publication extolled the four-story Prospect House, one of the 13.

> "The excellence of its wholesome table is recognized by its past patrons. Most of the guests are habitués whose yearly gathering resembles a large house party. The stranger, however, is certain of a cordial welcome, and the gleaming white exterior is a criterion of what may be expected within."
>
> "Business men will not find the hotel inconvenient, and the accommodations equal to those of any metropolitan hotel. Mail is sent and delivered regularly three times a day, and a long distance telephone is in the hotel office."

Hotel guests enjoyed croquet, bowling, tennis, walking, horseback riding, driving and "gala coaching parties." In the parlors, they encountered naturalists, poets, historians and writers such as Louisa May Alcott.

We drove to the 2,006-foot top of Wachusett Mountain where the old summit house once stood. In 1825 it became Mt. Adams to honor the newly inaugurated president, John Quincy Adams. The townsfolk staged a "grand celebration" with military parade, volleys of cannon fire and an immense bonfire on the summit to mark the change, but never embraced it. When Adams parted from the presidency, his name parted from the mountain.

The mountain now offered more than a view of the sunset or a fall pallet of New England foliage. It was skiing. Princeton natives have

continued as stewards of the mountain. In April 1996, *USA TODAY* reported:

> **Massachusetts, Princeton** – Bowing to pressure from environmentalists, the Watchusett Mountain Ski Area has abandoned plans to cut a trail through a stand of nearly 300-year old oaks.

"Coffee on the Common" at Gregory Hill was the sole breakfast option. It boasted perhaps the world's largest muffins. Blueberry, strawberry-rhubarb, and lemon poppy seed bulged out of their tins.

Six tables in a dining area were converted sewing machine bases, giving the old Singer treadle machines a new raison d'etre. The menu offered the option of baked beans or hashed brown potatoes with eggs, with pancakes or with French toast. Our waitress brought beans with my eggs and toast. On the way out, we liberated several muffins.

Three buildings of strikingly different architecture stand on the upper Common. The brick Victorian style Bagg Hall (1884) was the town hall.

The white, clapboard First Congregational Church (1838) with its lofty spire was a study in New England simplicity. Goodnow Memorial Building (1888) housed the public library. It was a two-story building of beige granite, with a clock tower. The clockwork mechanism was a series of gears, shafts, drums and cables. It seemed primitive but kept good time if wound once a week. That duty fell to a local man who spoke softly and carried a large hand crank.

Postmaster Anne Mason greeted us warmly. She was as delightful and informative as any postmaster could be. While talking about local history, she gave us a postcard showing a sketch of her family home, which was the site of the first post office in 1812. It read, "From the seventh great-granddaughter of the first postmaster."

We realized the local postal service had come a long way from the 1850 days of politically appointed Postmaster Moses Gill. (No relative of Anne's.) Gill didn't know what to do with material addressed to P.M. (i.e., Post Master), so he forwarded it to a local resident, Paul Mirick.

Back to the Common and library to seek more history. With the librarians' help we found tales such as:

> The disappearance of young Lucy Keyes in 1756, which remains unexplained. "Circumstantial evidence" originally pointed to Indians. A "troublesome" hermit, Littlejohn, was suspect. Or, perhaps she just wandered off. Her family became impoverished by their search for her.

The saga of Mary Richardson, the lone survivor of a Sagamore Indian attack on 37 settlers in 1776. She was held captive until age 10. John Hoas ransomed her at the now-celebrated Redemption Rock in Princeton.

The death of Captain Elisha Allen
whose grave marker read:

In memory of Capt. ELISHA ALLEN
who was inhumanly murdered by Samuel Frost
July 16th 1793
Aged 48 Years

Such a horrid murder we must
spare our readers the details.

We could have spent hours in this typical New England town looking for more history, but it was time to move on.

TRIP #7

Maine

"...no telling where it would have stopped."

...from the annual town report

Princeton, Maine
Population: 994
Breakfast for two: $10.00

Princeton, Maine, sits on the venerable U.S. 1 that stretches from Fort Kent, Maine to Key West, Florida. The town is a few miles from the St. Croix River that is the border between the U.S. and Canada. Timber, tourism and blueberries rule. Yes, blueberries. More than 90% of the nation's crop comes from surrounding barrens, yielding 30 million pounds a year of wild, low bush berries.

First stop was the library on Calais Road/U.S. 1, the only artery through the town. Grace Hiland had been librarian for less than two years. She was making improvements but one was still needed. The

library had no tele-
phone.

Grace let us sign
out a town history
for the evening.
Next day we found
a program for the
Congregational
Church 1958 centen-
nial celebration with
a plea scrawled
across the top: "I
wish he would shut

up." Was "he" the speaker, an unruly child, or a talkative adult?

At Grace's suggestion we checked in at the Lakeside Inn on Lewy
Lake, built in 1854. The Lakeside kitchen was the hub of activity. Conge-
nial hosts Charlie and Betty Field conducted business and had meals
there. Betty said when she married Charlie, she "liberated" him from his
home state of New Hampshire.

A "must-see" was the Princeton Regional Airport with its two 4,000-foot
asphalt runways. They accommodated sportsmen, an air taxi from Bangor
and Georgia Pacific's corporate jets. Originally, the unmanned terminal was
the relocated 1897 railroad depot building. Pilots logged takeoffs and land-
ings in a loose-leaf notebook.

Richard Howe greeted us from his mobile home near the airport.
He explained that the two cars in the tall grass belonged to "regulars"
who flew in for hunting and fishing. The "regular" who owned the
rusted, yellow mini-wagon had not been seen for three years.

At dinner in nearby Woodland we met Steve and Linda Croman. Steve had worked for Georgia Pacific, but was now a Maine Master Guide and Licensed Professional Forester. Of all the places he'd lived, including Alaska, he volunteered that this area was "the best."

We had breakfast at the Inn and it was a good one. So was the Irving Truck Stop where the lemon meringue pie and peach pie looked good and tasted even better. Where, we wondered, was native blueberry?

A carrier from the post office served 330 customers. Most of the 565 boxes were rented to the Passamaquoddy Indians since there was no delivery to their adjoining township. (Rachel Nicholes, a full bloodied Passamaquoddy, assured us that the term "Indian" was not offensive.) A sign outside advertised the "Hungry Tiger Take-out." With a "tiger" so close to the post office, we had no qualms having our cards postmarked there.

We met Fire Chief Donald Bailey outside the post office and enticed him into a photo with a fire engine.

In the town report he had written: "1995 was a good fire safe year...We responded to 32 calls...(One was) a call for a chicken coop fire at Paul Corbett's residence on 6/27/95 at 1:42 p.m.... I responded with Engine One and one untrained man. As we approached the scene, I could see that the coop was in the woods and there were trees burning. With very little manpower arriving, I decided to use the deck gun that was given us by Grand Island Stream Fire Dept. It saved the day... I was able to operate it by myself from the pumpdeck. Had the trees and Gilmore's old mill gotten going, there is no telling where it would have stopped."

Many of the towns' lumber mills succumbed to fire over time. The tannery and woolen mills built during the Civil War were history.

The lakes had been void of steamboats for decades. The last railroad engine pulled out 63 years ago. Despite these losses, pride and spirit sustained these rugged folks in Maine.

TRIP #8

Illinois
Iowa

"Four female rows to one male row."

...Chamber of Commerce President

Princeton, Illinois
Population: 7,197
Breakfast for two: $9.00 plus tip

M embers of the Hampshire Colony, like us, left Massachusetts for Illinois. They travelled by wagon, canal boat, sailing vessel, canoe and horse. Quite a contrast to our comfortable car and interstate highways. And they weren't greeted in 1830 by the sign proclaiming: "One of Illinois' Best Kept Secrets."

Many midwestern towns thrived during the first half of the 1900s but were bypassed by the Interstate Highway System and drained by migration to the cities. We quickly realized this Princeton was an exception. It melded residential, commercial and agricultural components into a thriving community. The Chamber of Commerce slogan, "Doing Things People Think Just Happen" suggested this was not by accident.

We could dwell on history and notables, including Elisha Lovejoy, William Cullen Bryant, Abraham

Lincoln and Ronald Reagan whose paths crossed the community, but on to other discoveries.

Canines were making news. The Friends of Strays needed money to keep their shelter open. Fleas also posed a nuisance but "Dog Dip Day," sponsored by the Tractor Supply Company, offered relief. The invitation read, "The owner will dip his/her own dog in a tank of 'Farnum Flea Stop Citrus Dog Dip' free of charge." The Chamber of Commerce sponsored a weekly "Brown Bag Day," when senior citizens could bundle their prescriptions for a pharmacist to sort out dangerous combinations. Also free.

The town was laid out in a grid and delineated in true American fashion, North Main Street and South Main Street. Its architecture was a mix of styles and time from Early Classical, Greek, Gothic Revival and Italianate to Neoclassical, Craftsman, Tudor and Prairie.

The Chamber of Commerce office displayed sample Super Bowl rings made by Jostens, a local company that also published yearbooks. The town's industrial roster listed 20 companies. Pioneer Hi-Bred, a leader in developing hybrid seed corn, started here in 1937. Heavy spring rains had made planting difficult. The female plants went in well, but the males had to be "mudded." I asked Chamber of Commerce President Don Allen, "What is the ratio of females to males?" When we met for an

after-work drink at the Elks Club, he answered, "Four female rows to one male row."

The Red Covered Bridge was built over Bureau Creek in 1863. It was one of five remaining from the 123 once in Illinois. It was the only one still used by cars. A sign warning, "FIVE DOLLARS FINE FOR DRIVING MORE THAN TWELVE HORSES, MULES OR CATTLE AT ONE TIME OR FOR LEADING ANY BEAST FASTER THAN A WALK ON OR ACROSS THIS BRIDGE." Most vehicles packed well over 12 "horses" but passed without challenge.

"Hoffman's" was undoubtedly the town's most unique business. It stocked over 8,000 discontinued China patterns to replace broken cups and plates. Allen Murphy, the 81-year-old proprietor, took over

his mother's antique shop 50 years ago and became enamored with china. 8,000,000 pieces were stocked in the shop, Murphy's home and barn, and his daughter and son's homes. A consultant estimated three years to computerize the inventory that only Murphy knew.

During breakfast at The Coffee Cup, waitress Mary Ann Smith made sure the cafe lived up to its name by keeping our coffee cups filled.

We were not surprised when the postmaster told us they often receive mail for other Princetons. The surprise came when he told about a recent visit by a woman who insisted she was in Princeton, Iowa. Not before he showed her the sign outside was she convinced that she was in the wrong state.

With a "Certificate of Appreciation" from the Chamber of Commerce and some day lily bulbs from 400 varieties at Hornbaker Gardens, we headed west to Iowa, knowing full well what state we had been in.

"It's tranquil and safe from bombers."

...a sales pitch to the UN

Princeton, Iowa
Population: 806
Breakfast for two: $9.75 plus tip

The Mississippi River ran smooth and wide at Princeton, Iowa. The town, with its homes, businesses and waterfront, stretched along the west bank below U.S. 67. West of the highway the land rose and became flat farmland planted in soy and corn. Today's laid-back community belied its youthful wildness.

Settlers first arrived in 1836. Two years later, a distillery was built. Early on two saloons along the river fueled the boatmen and raftsmen in a

"rowdy atmosphere." Women avoided the area. **B**usinessmen armed themselves.

The Sunrise Cafe was the local breakfast spot. Mary Gordon, best described as wiry, was owner, cook and waitress. On this day,

she waited tables and left cooking duties to her daughter-in-law. Mary's left wrist was in a green cast. Six weeks ago she unwisely demonstrated her skateboarding skills for her grandchildren. She fell and broke her wrist in three places. Undaunted, she planned to resume skateboarding, *and* rollerblading.

We took a table in the "linoleum room" where some regulars had preceded us. Our other choice was the "yellow carpet room." The cafe's regulars were as delighted with the friendly abuse they dished out as they were with the food Mary dished out. We were told that the six o'clock crowd of farmers was a better source of local news.

Mary Beth McGuire had been librarian since last year. Her enthusiasm made up for what the library lacked in volumes. It did have an unusual feature: a bank vault, now a children's reading room furnished with cushions. When the Old Farmers Savings Bank relocated across the street, it sold the building to the town for one dollar.

Penelope "Penne" Miller ("Penne," pronounced like the copper coin) was historian, artist, author, Lion, Princeton Day's organizer and consum-

mate collector. She bought the defunct two-story Pietchner's Grocery Building next to her home on River Drive just for her collections. Being visiting "dignitaries," we enjoyed an exclusive viewing of her collections of turtles, blue willowware, advertising signs and countless pieces of Americana. None was for sale.

South of Penne's home was Boll's general store. Merlin Boll's father started the business in the early 1900s. The groceries and dry goods downstairs included beer, soda, film, Pampers, nuts and bolts, toilet plungers, jeans, gloves and shirts.

Merlin invited us upstairs. The look in his eyes told us he missed the earlier days when the hall was a gathering place. Remnants showed it had been a ballroom, roller rink, basketball court, theatre and concert hall.

Some years ago, news was made when an Indian mound

containing nine skeletons and artifacts of the Hopewell culture, about 4,500 years old, was unearthed in a residential yard. Skeletal remains of a prehistoric zebra, maybe 45,000 years old, were also found under a street.

Julia Jensen McDonald's book about Iowa and Illinois communities described early 1900 residents Mack Hire, Job Dennis and Ed Martin as "lonely Democrats in a sea of Princeton Republicans." They consoled each other at Hire's clothing store, dubbed Princeton's Tammany Hall. In 1912, a Class of 1879 Princeton University graduate gave them hope. He was President-elect Woodrow Wilson (D).

Bill Wundram, *Quad-City Times* columnist, featured our visit in a front-page column, "If it's breakfast, this must be Princeton... DATE-LINE: Princeton, somewhere." He told us about a Princeton resident named Rogers who offered 300 acres of land to the United Nations for its headquarters after World War II. Rogers visited New York City several times to lobby for the site. His pitch, "It's tranquil and safe from bombers." It didn't sell.

Before leaving for St. Louis, we relaxed on a shaded bench overlooking the river. Billowy, white clouds and the distant, tree-lined shore

accentuated the river's blueness. The *Sierra Dawn* towboat pushed barges upriver while a Burlington Northern train thundered down the tracks. Neither made an effort to stop. In earlier days, they might have.

TRIP #9

Wisconsin
Minnesota
Michigan

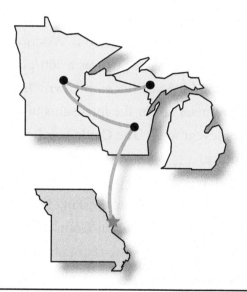

"The Beer with a Purr."

- Slogan for Tiger Brew, circa 1934

Princeton, Wisconsin
Population: 1,458
Breakfast for two: $6.35 plus 2-$1 C of C coupons plus tip

The hardware store sold T-shirts with two Holsteins and the greeting, "Welcome to Princeton, Wisconsin. You're Among Cows." The only cow we saw was a 500-pound Holstein made of concrete. It sold for $385 at Princeton Lawn Ornaments. Fences no longer protected premises "from the intrusions of cows which roamed the streets more of less at will." The Cattle Fair began in 1869 but now featured only produce.

The flea market billed as "Wisconsin's Largest Weekly Outdoor Event" was far more popular than the fair. Its 175 booths attracted upwards of 5,000 visitors every Saturday from late April to mid-October.

The flea market's popularity led to four antique malls and numerous

craft, antique and collectible shops. Husbands could play four golf courses minutes from downtown while their wives shopped.

"Where yesterday meets tomorrow" is how the *1996*

Business and Service Directory described "Princeton on the Fox." Tree-shaded homes, sans fences, and an old business district, purged several times at the turn of the century by fires, seemed more "yesterday" than "tomorrow."

The Fox River snaked through town, dividing the east and west sides. The divide was evident in the two cemeteries. Polish names dominated the Catholic cemetery on the west side where the Polish Catholic immigrants settled. In the city cemetery on the east side where German Protestant immigrants settled, headstones largely bore German names.

"Ripley's Believe It or Not" brought attention to the town when it featured the town's dentist, Dr. Joseph S. DRILL. In 1939, Princeton husband and wife team Martha and Ernest Hierstead created the first commercial version of the soft boots known as Muk Luks.

We stayed at Barnekow's Patio Motel on Pye Alley Road. Proprietor Harvey Barnekow told us Pye Alley

Pavilion once flourished across the street. During Prohibition young men brought buckets of "moon" from nearby stills to the dances. Their pell-mell exits from the pavilion when federal agents arrived were spectacular.

Lorraine Cederholm was the first librarian we had known who was called a "Pit Bull." For 30 years the library had been long cramped in an old general store. In 1980 Lorraine and others thought it time for a new facility. With $14.37 raised by a kids' lemonade and cookie sale, the campaign was started. They raised $49,000, matched by the state, and opened a new, paid-for building five years later. Their efforts were not without opposition as some in town petitioned against it and openly suggested Lorraine, not a native, go back to Milwaukee from where she came. Lorraine never backed off, earning the nickname, Pit Bull, from her colleagues.

We met Alice Crimmings in the library. She was born on 1-1-11. Alice's bright eyes and outspoken demeanor befit someone much younger. She confided that she wanted to live at least five more years to see what her daughters' children will be like because, "They're really stinkers now."

The local hardware store was once a theatre and Alice's father had

been a janitor when W. C. Fields once took the stage. After each run, her father brought home pictures of the stars. Neighborhood kids would eagerly await each new batch, which she and her sister posted gallery-like in their outhouse.

The Princeton Brewing Company was in a barn-like, brick building dated "J. Ernst—1894" on Farmer Street. The head of a heavily bewhis-kered tiger dominated the end of the building. Alice recalled her father saying that its beer sustained Polish wedding celebrations for days.

Prohibition closed the brewery but it resumed operations in 1934. Competition from the large Milwaukee breweries and legislated licensing fees made its revival short-lived. The brewery subsequently became a cheese factory, a mushroom factory and now an antique storage. What an ignominious fate for Tiger Brew, known locally for its "flavor and head" and advertised as "The Beer With a Purr."

Nancy Garner, our waitress at the M&M Family Restaurant, told us we just missed three regulars who always shared a table: an undertaker, the ex-police chief and a clergyman. Clearly, this was a local breakfast favorite. Nancy asked a customer if she wanted her "usual." The response, "Yes, please." Knowingly, Nancy gave the order to Mae the cook.

Outside the post office a man introduced himself as Paul Schlaefer, Piggly Wiggly Market manager and Chamber of Commerce president. He recognized us as "the couple on the Princeton prowl." News sure got around fast in this town,

Along the byways to Minnesota we saw some real cows.

"USED CARP"
...building sign

Princeton, Minnesota
Population: 3,719
Breakfast for two: $9.93 plus tip

We found the town layout an orderly grid with two exceptions. The main street, La Grande Avenue, whose name is far more pretentious than the town, ran diagonally across the grid. The Rum River wiggled through it. There were no vacant storefronts. People were going about their business.

We chose the Rum River Motel for its name. While dining at the Pine Loft, we noticed a room where trophies lining the head table tipped

us off to a sports banquet. Maybe golf? No, trap-shooting. It must have been an outstanding shooting group for everyone, perhaps 40, left with a trophy.

The K-Bob Cafe in downtown was the place for breakfast. It had operated under its present name since 1961 when the Tou family took over the K-Bob Soda Grill owned by Kay and Bob Hobert.

Marge Tou, in her early 80s, still helped out, but son Steve was the manager. Some

of the cafe signage still bore the original Soda Grill name. Marge explained that they couldn't afford a replacement sign when they bought the business. A recent $7,000 estimate convinced them that the old sign was fine. Besides, everyone knew what they served.

Conversation swirled around us. Off to the side some men were rolling dice to determine who paid for coffee. Steve told us it must be "OK" since the governor stopped by once and took his roll.

A World War II Sherman tank protected the Oak Knoll cemetery where Andrew and Bess Umbehocker rested with their eight children named alphabetically: David, Eve, Frank, Grover, Hilda, Irene Janice and Kenneth. Fitting in a cemetery whose flowery avenues were Arborvitae, Bittersweet, Carnation, Daisy, Evergreen, Forget-Me-Not, Goldenrod, Honeysuckle, Iris, Jonquil and Knob Cone Pine.

The Mille Lacs County Fairgrounds bordered the cemetery. No RIP on Friday night when stock cars *vroomed* around its speedway. The 105-year Mille Lacs County Fair had dirt track races for motorcycles and ATVs. Its quieter attractions included draft horse pulls, a talent show, camel rides, pig races and exhibits. This August, Pat Johnson had 96 exhibits, below her record 110. She exhibited in the garden, canned goods, baked goods and handicraft sections. Her whole wheat bread took

home a grand champion ribbon. Other ribbons, "according to her rough tally," were 50-plus blues (worth $1.50 each), 30-plus reds ($1.25) and six whites ($1).

The economy was originally based on furs. Timber, agriculture (potatoes for a short while), yellow bricks and dairies followed. Those earth-based industries diminished over time, changing the economic landscape. It now largely revolves around several hundred retail and professional service businesses. The industrial park housed kitchen cabinet finishers, sheet metal specialty products, spin metal products, office equipment and custom plastics.

There were some unique enterprises. "Princeton's Haul a Dog Inn" was a grooming and boarding facility, "A

Home Away From Home For Your Pet." Proprietor Audie Howe told us that he sometimes got calls seeking a reservation at the "Holiday Inn." Next to the "Dog Inn" was a large metal Quonset hut

with a white sign that read in two-foot letters "USED CARP." Fish? We wondered whether the "Princeton Off Sale Liquor" store ever had liquor "On Sale."

Princeton Area Chamber of Commerce secretary Corky Webb gave us the "Princeton Coloring Book & Tourism Guide." We deferred coloring illustrations of the Rum River Festival, the county fair, the nearby wildlife preserve, the Rum River and Green Lake, and the Christmas lighting which included one of the town's three water towers.

The city hall/Chamber/police station complex flew three flags, American, Minnesota and MIA-POW. The police station was unstaffed when we visited. Bev Hodges, city hall receptionist, had fielded two police calls. Good: two kids came in with a bicycle they found. Not so good: report of kids spray-painting windows at the new library.

Driving away we wondered whether some day "USED CARP" would welcome back "ARTS."

"...they even stole our dirt."

...a local historian

Princeton, Michigan
Population: 200
Breakfast for two: Courtesy of Steve Syrja

Princeton Mine Shaft #1 marked the approach to town. The shaft was long gone and no signs announced the town limits. So unknowingly we passed its scattering of homes and descended into Gwinn.

Thus, our first stop was the Forsyth Township offices where we met Karen Ketola, Beverly Kylma, Chic Hakes and Kelly Ussher. Karen lived in Princeton. Beverly had swapped her Princeton home with her son in Gwinn 25 years ago. Chic was the assessor and a member of the Emergency Medical Team. "Gets you out of the office," she said. Kelly made certain we spelled her name with a double "s." A "black sheep" of her family when ostracized dropped one "s" from Ussher, left town and was never heard from again.

Mining was once prominent in Princeton. Geologists first discovered iron in the area in 1844. From 1871 until the last mine closed in 1946, Princeton miners brought 3,221,588 tons of ore to the surface.

Frank Farquar's history described the early town as "rather a rough place and not much other enjoyment than drinking (took place), and the more they drank the more they would fight. A lot of drunks were tossed in the river, some never got out, but guess there was not much done about it."

The Forsyth Museum claimed night football was "invented" in Princeton in 1918 when the boys played in the light of carbide mining lamps on fence posts in Querino Piziali's yard. Pennsylvania was probably the site of the first night game 16 years earlier. But Princeton could still claim the first game played by the light of mining lamps.

Every Friday night at Jack's Hideaway, weather permitting, a dozen illuminated horseshoe courts hosted a co-ed tournament. No, mining lamps were not used. After the matches Jack's tavern business was brisk. Frequently, weather was not permitting. A record 251 inches of snow fell last year.

Protestant Finns and Italian Catholics lay in separate sections of the cemetery. Ethnic diver-

sity was evidenced by names in "Men of Steel," a booklet prepared by Ms. Morrissey's eighth grade students: Bianchi, Hahka, Maruke, Chickadarri, Ylonen, Poggi, Saari, Benaglio, Besola, Polini, Kuivinen, Arrieri, Juidici, Armatti, Sahi, Keskimaki, Sarasin, Vecellio, Negrinelli.

We had been put in touch with Russ Kanerva, an historian, and Steve Syrja, a free-lance writer. Russ volunteered a tour. Steve opened the Historical Museum and invited us for breakfast at his New Swanzy home. We accepted with provision for an "official" breakfast later by a Princeton road sign.

The "official" breakfast took place at the corner of Princeton Drive and Tapola Road. A hand-hewn log home built by Charlie Tapola served as background as we enjoyed a second helping of Steve's blueberry waffles (without syrup) and coffee.

Steve drove the tour "bus." Russ, armed with four albums, frequently routed it on long-abandoned roads. Shaft sites of old Princeton mines #1, #2 and #3 were obscured by undergrowth. Some places were posted with "Danger-Caving Ground, No Trespassing" signs. A deep water hole formed by a cave-in was near Princeton #2. It was believed to be the grave of an elderly man who disappeared several years ago.

An early boarding house site reminded us of a story in August 1926 *TRUE ROMANCES*. Its title: "A Determined Girl – The Adventures and Romance of an Immigrant Girl who Possessed Unconquerable Courage." Her romance blossomed when she met "him" in a Princeton boarding house.

William Gwinn Mather could be considered a "benevolent capi-

talist," but his benevolence doomed Princeton. By 1908 he was about to mine large lodes in the New Swanzy region, but he didn't want "a cluttering of non-descript buildings" around the mines. So he commissioned the "model town" of Gwinn on 400 ore-free acres.

Russ summed up the result. As Gwinn grew, it stole everything from Princeton: first the school, then the store, and nine years ago, the post office. Finally, they started hauling Princeton topsoil away. "Can you believe it, they even stole our dirt," he lamented.

And without a shred of guilt, a request to paint PRINCETON on the Forsyth Township water tower—which was in Princeton—had been ignored.

TRIP #10

Maryland
North Carolina
West Virginia
Tennessee

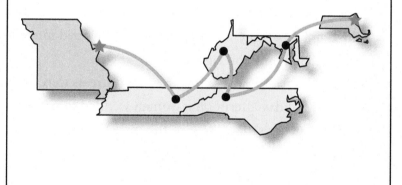

"Don't forget us."

...the elementary school principal

Princeton, Maryland
Population: 300 (est)
Breakfast for two: $1.05

L ittle did we expect when researching this Princeton that our experience at its elementary school would be a highlight.

In 1940 a plat was recorded for the Princeton Subdivision in a rural area of Prince George's County, Maryland. Section Two was taken for the Capital Beltway. Section One was developed into a neighborhood of about 80 homes on eight streets.

The single-story brick homes along tree-lined streets were unpretentious. On this fall Sunday afternoon a woman wedded to her Walkman was oblivious to our presence, as were the men tinkering on a car. A man was walking two Akitas whose anxiety over a dog chained to a tree was turning the walk into a tug-of-war. We hailed the "Walkman woman." As a 15-year resident, she assured us that some residents called the locale "Princeton."

We saw four police cars by the roadside. The officers were talking casually so we stopped. They had responded to a call about kids throwing stones at windows. The culprits, perhaps pleased at having attracted such force, had fled. One officer said she came from Kentucky and was familiar with its Princeton.

Princeton had no commerce, so our breakfast was outdoors, donuts and coffee on our car hood under a sign to the elementary school. Cars passed continuously but none stopped to inquire about our breakfast rite. Nor did they appear concerned that we were violating the "NO STOPPING OR STANDING" sign. The lack of curiosity and the absence of pick-up trucks confirmed that we were in suburbia, not a small town.

The elementary school was a sprawling one-story brick building with outdoor playing area. The children, accompanied by their teachers, walked to and from classes in orderly columns. "Remember, three (floor) tiles from the wall...take your hat off...we don't wear hats inside."

The fourth of five school rules read, "We will keep our hands and feet to ourselves." The children were a happy lot and never crossed the fine line between respect and regimentation in the classroom or in the cafeteria.

Principal Cynthia Rodgers was busy handling a minor discipline situation, checking on a student's bee sting (he was OK), arranging early dismissal for a student with a family issue and preparing to pick up her sick daughter at another school. Nevertheless, she told us about the school with enthusiasm worthy of a governor's visit.

The students were predominantly African American, many from Andrews Air Force Base families, which entitled the school to supplementary federal funding. Two-thirds of the school's 380 pupils qualified for free or reduced-priced lunches.

We kept our hands to ourselves while we were escorted to Susan Clifford's classroom. Once there, we described our Princeton visits to a third and a fourth grade class. The kids were not bashful asking questions: "Have you been in New York?" Our answer, "Yes." A response, "I have an uncle who lives there." "Chicago?" "Yes." "My cousin lives there." "St. Louis?" "Yes, that's where we live." "My aunt is there." Mention of St. Louis pleased Susan because a forthcoming lesson about mid-America included a "stop" in St. Louis at the Gateway Arch.

We switched our geography lesson to China where we had been 14 times since 1984. It became apparent that these ten-year-old Air Force kids had travelled far more than many adults. Hands raised and questions flowed about Italy, Philippines, England, Germany and Saudi

Arabia. Their enthusiasm didn't wane with our parting lesson in Chinese, *xie xie* (thank you) and *zai jian* (goodbye). Uninhibited efforts produced credible pronunciations as each student filed past us when the class was dismissed. Susan described her teaching approach as a blend of firmness and warmth. "Firmth," she called it.

Back at the office, Cynthia bid us goodbye with hugs and added, "Don't forget us!" How could we?

"Corn, tobacco, cotton, beans, hogs and poultry" "And kids."

...couple at A&A Coffee Shop

Princeton, North Carolina
Population: 1,181
Breakfast for two: $8.85 plus tip

A sign by a cotton field gave us a choice: left to Dead End Road or right to Princeton. We chose the latter and found a town of broad streets and modest homes. The *Johnston County Visitors Guide* listed Powell Gardens as its only attraction

Hurricane Fran had swept through a month before. Power outages

lasted up to ten days. Much of the damage was cleared, but there was still evidence of the storm's strength; fallen trees by the water tower, truckloads of branches and corrugated tin roofs peeled off rural buildings.

In neighboring Selma, we were told to seek out the "B & B" eatery in Princeton. It proved elusive so we inquired at the Town Hall about a breakfast place. There was one, but it was "A & A."

A sign advertising COBLE Ice Cream over "A & A Coffee Shop" hung outside. The shop was typical of small town cafes with booths, tables in the middle and a counter fronting the grill. Sherry Weaver, who lived a few doors away, brought us coffee. Our choice of local smoked ham with our eggs was a good decision. We were not surprised when grits appeared on our plates. Potatoes were 75 cents extra.

Tom and Lee Holloman sat in the next booth. They planned a leisurely breakfast and "for excitement" a drive to Smithfield to shop. When asked about area farm products, Tom volunteered, "Corn, tobacco, cotton, beans, hogs and poultry." Lee added quickly, "And kids."

Jackie Matthews, a lifelong resident, was the morning cook. She had been a waitress for 24 years and for four years a cook at the "A & A." She told us it stood for Arnett & Aycock. Jackie sported a tattoo on her ankle. She sent us on our way with a paper cup of local grapes and "Y'all come back."

The town was originally known as Boon Hill. In 1845, North Carolina Railroad sent the first train through town. Today, Norfolk Southern freight trains pass on tracks along the main street. The Civil War didn't affect the town until Sherman's troops burned homes and destroyed farms. The local "teacherage," a name given in yore to the living quarters of single, female teachers, was recently torn down after years of disuse.

Ava Gardner was born near Smithfield and lived there until she left for Hollywood in 1941. She was remembered as "the down-to-earth country girl from Johnston County." The County Arts Council operated the Ava Gardner Museum. Supporters were known as "Ava Advocates."

Town Hall clerk Jean Gurley and secretary Deborah Kornegay took us under their wings. They introduced us to the young two-term mayor, David Holt, who managed a general supply store called A. F. Holt & Sons, Inc. The Holt name went back before the town's founding. The store was a block from Town Hall, which made access to the mayor convenient and occasionally distracted him from business.

Police Chief Rick Massengill was in his thirties and had been chief for four years. At Town Hall, a young boy with his mother spotted Rick and asked for a "badge." The sticker Rick put on the lad's shirt evoked a broad smile. Rick frequently stopped his patrol car to "pin" them on children. His badges apparently bestowed a degree of prestige and helped create, as Rick hoped, a police-friendly community.

This Princeton was truly a friendly town. Everyone we passed greeted us. Wayne James, pastor of Grace Independent Baptist Church, struck up a conversation as we mailed our cards at the post office. Judy Talton, branch manager of the bank, introduced her four tellers and rushed out as we were leaving to give us a "Welcome to Princeton" brochure. The *Johnston County Visitor Guide* would have been well advised to add "Friendly People" as a town attraction.

"In recognition of Outstanding Efforts to Promote Princetons Everywhere"

...Chamber of Commerce

Princeton, West Virginia
Population: 7,043
Breakfast for two: $10.22 plus tip

John Denver made West Virginia and country roads synonymous but the roads serving this Princeton were anything but country. Thanks to Interstate 77 and U.S. 460 it was a major transportation center. It was part of the much larger Bluefield micropolitan area. Still, the city had a small town ambience.

We stopped at the Princeton-Mercer County Chamber of Commerce. Our odyssey sparked the interest of the executive assistant. In short order we had a wealth of information that included H. W. Straley's *Memoirs of Old Princeton*, which offered some intriguing historical notes.

PRINCETON
Scene of several actions, May, 1862, between Federal troops from General Cox's army and Confederate forces under Jenifer and Wharton. When the Confederates abandoned their camp here, the town was set on fire and partially burned.

"Foots" Coleman, the 96-year-old resident of Princeton, Arkansas, would likely have termed them "Stories and Lies."

In 1862, a Confederate detachment was protecting provisions in the courthouse. When its commander, a Captain Jenifer, heard that Federal forces were approaching, he ordered the town torched and fled. Most of the town burned. One home owned by an English lady was spared. It seems the Confederates wanted to avoid "international complications with Great Britain."

Mrs. McNutt's home survived the fire but was looted. Outraged, she asked a Federal officer, "Major McKinley, I would like to know whether or not there are any gentlemen in the Yankee army?" He politely raised his hat and replied, "Madam, I pass for one in Ohio, and I shall see at once that these annoyances cease." The gentlemanly major became our 25th president.

At the Battle of Pigeon Roost the Federal troops suffered far more casualties than the Confederates. Apparently, German troops among them had lost their fighting edge when they emptied a keg of whiskey captured before the battle.

Frank James thought of robbing the Bank of Princeton. After seeing its dilapidated appearance, he decided otherwise. Little did he know that the old leather trunk contained $25,000 in gold. Another version suggested that the bank vice president, a Civil War veteran, had hosted him at dinner. Frank and Jesse generally bypassed banks run by ex-confederates.

Princeton won by a landslide the 1906 election against Bluefield to retain the county seat. One Princeton precinct of 150 eligible voters miraculously cast 818 votes.

At Bobby Jo's Cafe, Carla Wellman greeted us for breakfast with, "How y'all doing?" Though we declined biscuits and gravy, she told us that her husband liked her grandmother's gravy; she likes her own; her five-year old son liked both.

Beth Harmon sat nearby and informed us that she was a member of AARP. She ate here frequently and sang regularly for the Methodist Home residents. Harold Buckner, Democrat candidate for Sheriff, stopped to shake hands and didn't seem to care that he was talking to out-of-staters.

The Old Town walking tour listed 26 points of interest. Ten of those were on Walker Street. Most noteworthy was the Mercer County Courthouse. The

Wiley Cabin and Broyles Cabin weren't on the tour but both had been faithfully restored. On the same plot was a unique structure, a "four-holer." This 150 year-old outhouse was originally in North Carolina, then moved here. It was no longer in working order. A West Virginia Department of Health bulletin described it as a "Sanitary Pit Privy, Wood Floor and Riser Type." The bulletin also advised: "Every privy should be located below and as far as possible from any water supply, such as a well or spring."

A surprise awaited back at the Chamber. Executive Director George Santon invited us to be guests at the Chamber directors' meeting at the Roma III Pizzeria & Restaurant. Reporters were there from the *Princeton Times* and *The Observer*. Mayor Anita Caldwell gave us souvenirs of the city and Chamber President Rick Kephart presented us

with "The Visitor's Award." It read: "In Recognition of Outstanding Efforts to Promote Princetons Everywhere." We humbly offered our thanks for the award and the gracious hospitality they and others had shown us.

"We're not southerners. We're mountaineers."

...Longtime resident

Princeton, Tennessee
Population: 1,000 est.
Breakfast for two: $3.26 plus tip

Some Princetons, we learned, required a bit of sleuthing. The *Rand McNally Commercial Atlas* listed a Princeton in the Johnson City area of northeast Tennessee. Road maps did not show its location. The Johnson City Chamber of Commerce did not recognize its existence but acknowledged a Princeton Road in the city.

With that scant information we travelled to Johnson City. Princeton

Road was, in fact, a major thoroughfare. We followed a sign to the Princeton Arts Center, passing Princeton Square, Princeton Lane, Princeton Medical Center, Princeton Plaza and a few other Princeton "somethings" en route.

We met Arts Center Coordinator Lisa Musgrove, and BINGO— Rand McNally was right! There was a Princeton, Tennessee. Lisa produced *The Princeton Story, Its School and Commu-*

nity by Frances Dugger Rowan, now a California resident. Frances and her sister had stopped by the center two years ago. The old brick building that was once their school inspired Frances to preserve its history.

We were aware of the local accent, so we knew by George Pimental's accent he came from elsewhere. His 26 years in the Johnson City area had not dulled his distinctive Boston accent. George volunteered at the center. He and two colleagues published *The Laffs & Times of Mt'n Dewey* in which Mt'n Dewey weaves tall tales with a Tennessee twang. Having taught ESL (English as a Second Language) in China, we decided George had mastered TSL (Tennessee-ese as a Second Language).

Early Princeton was made up largely of farmland. Most had given way to light commerce, condominiums and homes. To the east stood

Masters Knob, a formidable hill. Its trees were once the source of bark for a tannery. To the south was a farm with four horses in its meadow.

While exploring, we saw Louise McKinney at her mailbox on Princeton Road. The retired librarian invited us in. She was now known as the "Cat Lady." The title seemed apt. She had 17 cats in a large fenced area. She reminisced about Princeton for over an hour until her hair appointment prompted a halt. As we left, she said, "I hope you've learned one thing about us in Princeton. We're not southerners. We're mountaineers."

Louise arranged a visit with David Swadley whose family went "way back." His great-grandfather gave the land for the first school and had a peach orchard on Masters Knob. David was born in a log cabin nearly 80 years ago and had lived in his present home since 1951. He volunteered that he was an anemic boy and "weak in the legs," but "filled out" when he played football in high school.

The night of our arrival we ate at the "Crazy Tomato," an Italian eatery on Princeton Road. It had Iranian owners, a Mexican cook and a southern waitress. When Kim Ward, the southern waitress, couldn't come up with a suggestion for our "Breakfast in Princeton" the following day, she summoned co-owner Tony Rahrow. His solution: "Stop in tomorrow before mid-morning opening hours. I'll tell the cook to make breakfasts."

We entered the "Crazy Tomato" the next morning by the employees' door. Cynthia Fiumara, the noonday waitress and fittingly Italian, was unaware we were stopping by, but she adjusted. Without ordering, our breakfast appeared: well-fried eggs and toast made from pizza dough. With no breakfast menu, Cynthia puzzled over the bill but eventually came up with a price. Since Princeton had never incorporated and its geography was vague, we decided on a backup breakfast of coffee and donuts outside the Arts Center.

The identity of the Princeton community had diminished so much since mid-century that few were aware of its past. Development of its remaining open land and time would soon complete its integration into Johnson City. We were fortunate to visit with the remaining few who could share their recollections.

TRIP #11

Alabama
Georgia (Rockdale County)
Georgia (Clarke County)
South Carolina
Florida

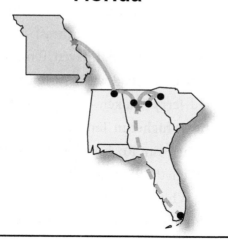

"That was no fun."

...crestfallen high school boy

Princeton, Alabama
Population: 250
Breakfast for two: $8.45

Travelers didn't seek out Princeton in northern Alabama, the exceptions being the couple from Princeton, British Columbia, who visited ten years ago, and of course, the Perrys. The nearest sizeable city was Scottsboro, 25 miles southeast.

We entered Alabama from a well-paved Tennessee road and found ourselves on a rough, narrow road without shoulders. "Why the difference?" we later asked Jerry Walker, our host at Flying Heart Ranch. "Taxes, they're five times higher in Tennessee."

Princeton was in the Paint Rock Valley and north of the Paint Rock River that snaked through the 25-mile valley. Cattle and horses grazed in the valley's meadows. White tail deer and eastern wild turkeys ventured down from the hills to browse. Corn, hay and soybeans were grown in small quantities. Hardwood was harvested from the mountains.

The lodge's main room was a gallery of preserved wildlife. It displayed three racks of antlers, two whitetail deer heads, a roebuck head and more antlers, two hawks, one curlew and two Caperceil grouse. Jerry had operated inns near Laconia, New Hampshire, and in Nantucket, Massachusetts. He created the Flying Heart from an old house and 53 acres of

farm property he purchased in 1992.

Jerry was a 73-year old retired army colonel. He clarified his marital status by referring to his "then-wife." His four daughters were college graduates and on their own. He had recently found companionship when Jerry, a Red Tick Hound, wandered onto the ranch. (There are also Blue Tick Hounds.) Jerry, the dog, had been maltreated, so Jerry, the innkeeper, took Jerry, the dog, to Jerry, the veterinarian, who patched him up.

We had breakfast at the ranch. Its specialty, French toast made with batter prepared the night before to allow proper aging, was exceptional. The view of the woods from the dining area created the "quiet escape" the ranch advertised.

During breakfast Jerry, the dog, had disappeared. Jerry, the innkeeper, was concerned that Jerry, the dog, would get into the bad habit of chasing deer. So, in

unmilitary fashion he called out "Din-din, din-din!" Jerry, the dog, reappeared and soon was eating "din-din" from his bowl.

The town center consisted of a post office, several homes, two abandoned general stores, an unused garage and the volunteer fire department. A variety of homes and several churches were on the two roads from the center. In affluent communities, rusty old cars in yards would be considered an eyesore. Here, they seemed to enhance the southern ambiance.

Activity in town was minimal. There was a bit of coming and going at the post office. The only significant activity on a Tuesday morning was at the Paint Rock Valley School. A bus driver carried a pail of water to two yellow buses. He smiled and explained, "Gotta slop the hogs."

School secretary Loretta Harris was a native. Her coworker Jane Money came from Maine and teacher Charlotte Paton from New Jersey.

Assistant Principal and agriculture science teacher Tim White greeted us, and then disappeared to the principal's office. The principal was in the Bahamas.

We noticed two boys solemnly enter the principal's office one by one where Tim held court, so to speak. Each boy soon departed even more crestfallen. One muttered, "That was no fun."

The two lads thought playing basketball in the gym would be more fun than attending class. They also figured—wrongly—that the substitute teacher wouldn't report them. That led them to choose corporal punishment (i.e., paddling), legal in Alabama, instead of a three-day suspension. Short-term suffering at the hands of the assistant principal was perhaps wiser than harsher punishment from their parents.

Jerry, the innkeeper, gave us a two-hour tour of the area. When we returned to the ranch, Jerry, the dog, was waiting. We bid goodbye to both Jerrys, drove across the one-way bridge that spanned the Paint Rock and headed to Georgia.

"Never heard of it."

…Conyers Chamber of Commerce and others

Princeton, Georgia-Rockdale County
Population: 60
Breakfast for two: $5.82 plus tip

The AAA map showed a Princeton in Rockdale County about seven miles northeast of Conyers and we chose to believe it. Rand McNally did not list this Princeton. The Conyers Chamber of Commerce and county historical society had both replied politely, "Never heard of it." This would become a familiar refrain.

We paid a premium for the last available Conyers motel room. The influx of people coming to witness Nancy Fowler's monthly vigil had literally left no rooms at the inn. Conyers, a city of about 10,000, was undisturbed until six years ago when Fowler claimed the Virgin Mary

had appeared to her. Since then, thousands had come seeking a sighting. *The Rockdale Citizen* reported at the fifth anniversary of Fowler's first sighting that over 12,000 pilgrims had

visited her farm, in 1,950 vehicles, 46 motor homes, 85 chartered buses and 90 cabs. Fowler "received" her visions inside her home. Pilgrims waited outside for status reports.

The Conyers library reference assistant Holly Heilman had "never heard of it," but she found seven references that might reveal Princeton did exist. Pay dirt! A paragraph on page 81 of The History of Rockdale County entitled "PRINCETON:"

"Princeton was located near Salem Baptist Church, and was the site of the first school in the community. This was a one-room school for grades one through eight, all taught by the same teacher. The school was also attended by children around Costley's Mill and Dial Mill nearby. There was also a cotton gin, run by Mr. George Sammons, and a 'General Store' kept by Mr. Will Sammons at this location."

The Salem Baptist Church was dedicated in 1830 and still in use. During the Civil War, services became "irregular" and the church gradually dissolved. Local lore described "Uncle" Isaas [sic] Eubanks walking

"six or so miles" to conduct services, some at which he was the lone attendee. Neighbors apparently moved by "Uncle" Isaas' dedication, began to join him and eventually the church was reborn.

Costley's Mill ceased operations in 1973 when many of the buildings burned. Bev and Syl Bowman bought the land and surviving buildings. Bev, who "never heard of it," told us how they created the present theme park, Costley's Mill Park. The 450-foot raceway, chute and stone foundations were the only remnants of the mill.

It seemed that any town with a gristmill in Sherman's path boasted a heroine who saved the mill. This Princeton had good ole Aunt Minnie Puckett.

"Aunt Minnie implored the Federals not to burn the (grist) mill because it was the community's only means of support," reported one account. Another reported "Mrs. Puckett sacked all the flour in the mill and put sacks in the mill pond. The flour that got 'wet caked' protecting that within which remained dry. She then sowed the wheat that was on hand over the fields." Her plea (or fib) succeeded as Sherman's soldiers spared the mill and marched on.

We asked Sheriff Deputy Hamby at Donna Marie's Pizza and Pasta Restaurant in Conyers about breakfast possibilities in Princeton. He had "never heard of it" but knew the area we described and suggested Porky Joe's just west of Salem Baptist Church Road.

The Princeton School had been located across from Porky Joe's. Owner Chris Clanton and customers had "never heard of it." In the morning farmers, service workers, truckers and policemen chose their breakfast from a list of 11 biscuit and gravy combinations. We had the traditional sausage gravy, naturally with grits.

Historical society Co-President Dale Brown, whose first response was "never heard of it," was curious and confirmed later that there had been a Princeton School and settlement along the very route he drove every weekday.

Nobody had heard of this Princeton. Its identity had been hidden in a history book. After our visit, a few more had heard of it.

"So what was a Yankee doing here...in 1832?"

...April 1990 Athens Magazine

Princeton, Georgia-Clarke County
Population: 300
Breakfast: $4.45 for pastries for four

In 1833 a group of eight men bought 62½ acres on the Middle Oconee River that included two mills and named it the Cramak Manufacturing Company. A year later the name was changed to Princeton Factory. The word "Factory" was dropped by 1866. One historian claimed Princeton was never incorporated but *Clarke County, Georgia and the City of Athens* (1893) by George Morton Straham stated otherwise:

"The town of Princeton is incorporated and has a population of 225...It takes its character from the presence of the cotton mill, in which most of the inhabitants are employed. Two stores, a school, a church and Sunday school and a blacksmith shop are also found at this (time)."

Years later, the town was brought into the Athens city

limits and identified as the Princeton District of Clarke County. A historian noted in 1965 that "on highway maps of the various oil companies, the 'town' of 'Princeton' is still shown although this is in error."

The area was considered less than desirable when the mill was in operation. Recently, the Princeton Mill subdivision became a choice place to live.

William E. Williams, the factory's first president, came from Princeton, New Jersey (Princeton University Class of 1806). A question about this outsider in the April 1990 *Athens Magazine*: "So what was a Yankee doing here in Athens in 1832, holding a position of such high esteem?" Author Luke Ferguson answered, "It seems that it was not uncommon for southerners to import industrial know-how from wherever they could find

it—even if it was from New Jersey."

The mill processed cotton and wool. Over the years it had ups and down and changes in ownership. It was last sold in 1943 to O. W. Haygood who

installed a gasoline-powered gristmill for corn. Locals recalled the smell of heated corn mash. Ferguson observed, "Perhaps it is only a coincidence that a nearby establishment at times had a supply of 'white lightning.'" The mill ceased operation in 1965. It was gutted by fire in 1973.

Our initial contact, Sis Budd, at the Convention and Visitors Center told Barbara Middleton, a subdivision resident, why two strangers would be tramping through the valley behind her home to explore the mill ruins. Barbara was game for the adventure and was waiting for us at the subdivision. She decided that Marguerite Burch's home had the best access to the mill.

We asked Marguerite if we could use her backyard the next morning as a route down for a mill-side coffee and donut "Breakfast in Princeton." Marguerite's answer, "Of course," was followed by the suggestion that we bring the donuts and she and husband Charlie would provide coffee in

their dining area overlooking the mill ruins. This was truly "the kindness to strangers," especially when both had morning appointments and were leaving for Florida in the afternoon.

We upgraded our part of the breakfast with pastries from the Black Forest Bakery. Marguerite supplemented the coffee with orange juice and a fresh fruit bowl. Charlie, a retired banker, returned in his red pick-up from a morning prayer meeting to complete our breakfast foursome.

Conversation centered on family, their recent marriage (both had been widowed) and, of course, Princetons.

Our descent to the mill ruins was slow. Fallen leaves, clay soil and brick debris made for tricky footing. The Middle Oconee was a trickle at the time of the year we visited. The remaining brick walls of the mill were partially hidden in the heavily wooded vale. Pulleys, a drive shaft, a turbine and twisted iron components remained. There were few traces of the mill's 15-foot dam. The subdivision and dense woods screened the ruins of the mill's eroding remnants.

As we left for South Carolina we realized the story of this Princeton was not one of today but of yesterday.

"Memories belong on walls, not in albums."

...life-long Princeton resident

Princeton, South Carolina
Population: 100
Breakfast for two: Courtesy of Joe McCullough

We had a friend in Princeton, South Carolina, before our visit, in "gentleman farmer" Joe McCullough, courtesy of the Anderson County Chamber of Commerce. Before we left, we had another friend, Agnes Babbs.

Prior to our trip, we called Joe about a breakfast spot and lodging in Princeton. "We have both," he said. He would be glad to join us for a country breakfast and guaranteed we'd "be really full when we left."

Next day, Joe called us. He was curious how we came by his name, or so he said. And by the way, he lived alone and had seven bedrooms and four baths. The down side, "I don't cook." Regardless, we accepted his invitation to stay at his home overnight.

We drove into Princeton on U.S. 25. The town was largely a scat-

tering of dwellings and businesses along this north-south route. The largest commercial enterprise was the expansive Hot Spot truck stop. It employed 50 people, probably more than all the other town enterprises combined.

Joe was a retired dairy farmer and now a real estate agent. He also volunteered as a game warden, carrying arms when on duty. Other times he kept his weapons at home, which probably made him secure when total strangers like us stayed overnight. Not that we looked menacing.

We assured our own security by choosing a room with a life-sized cutout of John Wayne.

A sign at the entrance to Joe's large, brick ranch-type home read: "Cedarhurst Farms, McCullough." It listed the names of his seven children

hanging one below the other on separate shingles.

McCulloughs had been here about two hundred years. They once owned 2,000 acres, grew cotton and had seven tenants. Joe still had 500 acres. His herd was down to 50 Holsteins. His grandfather, Colonel James McCullough, commanded the 16th Regiment of South Carolina Volunteers during the Civil War and was buried in the tree-shaded family plot in the meadow.

Joe was right. We were "really full" when we finished our country breakfast with grits, of course, at the Princeton Family Restaurant.

Joe's royal tour included the Possum Kingdom Fire Department. His Jeep Wagoneer ran smoothly in spite of its 352,700 miles. Joe had been twice widowed. On the dashboard of the Jeep were photos of the "two wonderful ladies" he had lost.

We spent a morning hour with Joe's friend, 74-year-old Agnes Babbs. She was a lifelong resident and been a high school teacher for 41 years. Her father had established the Babb General Store along the

highway in 1921. It was once a prosperous business, but all that remained were brick walls.

Agnes was getting around quite well while recovering from two knee replacements. She pointed out the many photos on her living room wall by saying, "Memories belong on walls, not in albums! I look at them every morning and enjoy them."

Joe and Agnes were a wealth of information on local lore—

On Route 25 (and baseball):

Used to be a speed trap. My dad's brother George Babb and Charlie Davenport hid in a barn and "trapped" unsuspecting tourists. – **Agnes**

During work on a section by my farm, elderly Mr. Gaines stopped to inquire about a welding job. The visit was approaching 30 minutes when I questioned him about a rag in his pocket. "Oh," he said, "some guy gave it to me as I drove into the work area below your farm." Cars were lined up for miles, futilely waiting for the flag exchange. I sent Mr. Gaines, flag in hand, back to highway and retreated inside. **– Joe**

When I was young the highway was part of the outfield. I recall one Saturday afternoon traffic was so slack the game was never interrupted by a passing car. **– Agnes**

On Babb General Store:

We stocked everything but coffins and even considered building a shed for them. The Mills Brothers once sang there promoting Morton's Salt. In 1935 the Standard (Oil Company) News featured the store's new canopy and gas pumps. **– Agnes**

On local characters:

Rafe Martin, a rather mean-spirited person, had a disagreement with a man who died while driving away from a party with him. Rafe claimed the man was killed when the car ran off the road. The authorities

concluded differently when they found a fatal bullet in the deceased's body.
– Agnes and Joe

One day before blinker signals old Mr. Davis turned off the highway toward his home without giving a hand signal. When Davis stopped, a driver following him demanded, "Why didn't you give a signal?" "Why?" asked Mr. Davis, "Everyone knows where I live." – **Agnes and Joe**

On wildlife:

I was never a hunter but once shot a deer that had been badly injured by a car. I showed the mounted head and won second prize for the season's largest rack. – **Joe**

This year, a doe that lived in the woods behind my house had triplets. A rare occurrence. (Cows had triplets once in eight million births; deer maybe less frequently.) In the evening the doe brings her three offspring to join other deer at my salt lick. – **Joe**

I was big on bass fishing, travelling widely for the best fishing. With pricey rods and a bass boat, my biggest catches were nine and ten-pounders. My son caught an eleven-pounder in the pond just behind our house. – **Joe**

Things hadn't always gone well for Princeton, South Carolina. The now idle Ridgeway Gin once turned out 3,000 bales of cotton a year. The railroad planned through Princeton ran out of money and the tracks were laid eventually, but ten miles away. Honea Path absorbed the post office some years ago. The beavers kept rebuilding their dam across Lime Creek. But as Agnes said, "I pretty well like it here. I'm satisfied; maybe too satisfied." And we know Joe felt the same.

" 'Duck'...had... influence"

...1909 Quindecennial Record of the Princeton Class of 1894

Princeton, Florida
Population: 2,400
Breakfast for two: $9.48 plus tip

The seeds for Princeton, Florida, were sown when Gaston "Duck" Drake, Princeton University Class of 1894, left the university after his junior year for "business reasons" and returned to Florida.

By 1904, he had bought and moved a lumber mill to South Miami-Dade County. He built a company town complete with a commissary, over 100 homes for married workers, a boarding house for single men and "quarters" for black workers. He painted *all* the buildings orange and black to honor his university.

From the 1909 Quindecennial Record of the Princeton Class of 1894:

"'Duck' is the real thing in the Drake Lumber Company in Miami... He had sufficient influence to secure...a post office at the company's mill and to have it named 'Princeton.'"

When timber ran out, the mill closed in 1923 and Princeton evolved into a "sleepy farming community" and "crossroads" for some of the country's largest produce farms. Crops included pole beans, boniatos, tomatoes, sweet corn, cucumbers, zucchini squash (not my favorite), avocados,

papayas and malanga.

Princeton was on U.S. 1, also known as the Federal Highway, and on this stretch, the Dixie Highway. Town limits signs fell victim to Hurricane Andrew in 1992 and had not been replaced. Constant traffic flowed on the highway where the Drake Lumber Company had been. Motels, strip malls, fast food restaurants and small businesses stood between the highway and small bungalows, a mobile home park, commercial nurseries and vegetable farms. The only orange and black was at a paint testing station where racks of color chips were exposed to the strong ultraviolet rays of the Florida sun.

At a Pancake House, Mike and Deb Desmond shared their "Andrew experience." The leading edge of Andrew had passed their home and

the calm of the eye allowed damage inspection. Mike reported that food would be available, in the form of avocadoes. Their backyard was a foot deep in the green fruit, blown from a nearby grove. When the trailing edge passed, Mike reassessed the food supply. Not one avocado remained, nor were any in sight.

Biscuits and gravy were not available for breakfast at Rosy's Grill. Rosy offered $1 tacos instead. Framed pictures of eggs assured us that she served our preferred fare. Our waitress Debbie Dambrosio found her Spanish necessary, not for us, but for staff and other customers. Upon leaving, we noticed a window sign: "MENUDO $5.00." We feared we had missed a new breakfast treat. That was until we learned "MENUDO"

was a hot, spicy soup made of pig intestines and stomach.

Before arriving, we had contacted Daniel Adams, a retired sergeant major. He recalled with amusement that, as a member of an Inspector General's audit team in Wyoming, he was always the center of attention. He was convinced he was the only black person ever seen in those parts.

Andrew had destroyed Daniel's home, which he rebuilt. The Princeton and Naranja communities bonded, but with FEMA aid coming slowly, Daniel formed a committee to speed it up and to focus on common needs. It was so successful that under his leadership it was formalized as the Pronceton/Naranja Community Council.

Driving to Daniel's home we saw another view of Princeton. Neat pastel stucco homes were laid out with geometric precision. There were some palm trees. Properties were well cared for. We learned that these neighborhoods were unfortunately becoming prey to robberies, sometimes in daylight, and encroachment of drug traffic from the Miami area.

The influx of immigrants was rapidly changing the town's character, just as the mill and its workers did in the early 1900s, the doomed railroad to the Keys in the 1920s, construction of U.S. 1 in the 1930s, Homestead Air Force Base in the 1940s, and hurricanes over the century. No doubt there will be more changes and hurricanes in its future.

New Jersey

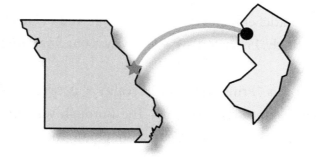

"Crepes aux fraise et aux framboises"

...the 32nd breakfast

Princeton, New Jersey
Population: 12,100
Breakfast for two: Guests of Princeton University President Shapiro

An Arkansas historian called it the "grand pappy of them all." It was by far the largest Princeton. Senior to the next oldest by 35 years. Battlefield, university or borough, and the name source of 12 others. Fittingly, Princeton, New Jersey, was our final "Breakfast in Princeton, USA."

On the map it is "Princeton," but in reality it is two, the Borough of Princeton and Princeton Township. The Borough was the original town. Locals described it as the hole of a doughnut, the ring being the

Township. The Borough, incorporated in 1813, was our "Breakfast in Princeton" location.

A recent referendum to consolidate the two into one failed—again. Regardless, the two melded affluent and middle class residential areas, abundant trees, educational centers, research industries, corporate headquarters, and consumer and service businesses that thrived in the upscale environment.

We had sent President Harold T. Shapiro a Nassau Hall postcard from each Princeton. We invited him and his wife to join us for our New Jersey breakfast. His return invitation to their home, Lowrie House, was too gracious to refuse.

President Shapiro greeted us at the stately Italianate designed Lowrie House. He presented us with a gift of Don Oberdorfer's *Princeton University, The First 250 Years*. It was a princely gift and a perfect addition to baseball caps, mugs, pins and souvenirs we had received in other Princetons. Tom Wright, a university vice president, and Marcia Snowden, the president's assistant, joined us.

This gourmet breakfast was quite a contrast to the coffee and donuts on the hood of our car in the smaller Princetons we visited along the highways and byways. The final "Breakfast in Princeton" consisted of orange juice and fresh fruit for a start; crepes aux fraises et aux framboises for the entree; petite muffins and coffee on the side. The table in a windowed-alcove was set with a linen tablecloth and napkins, fine china and patterned silverware. It was my only "coat and tie" break-fast. My usual attire (plaid shirt and chinos) would have been, as

George Gobel once said, "as out of place as brown shoes with a tuxedo."

President Shapiro looked at our albums and recounted a childhood vacation when his family drove cross-country, deliberately taking small town routes. Vice President Wright, a native North Carolinian, relived his younger days as he looked at North Carolina photos. Breakfast ran well beyond President Shapiro's first morning meeting. Mrs. Shapiro had sent her apologies for being away.

The lack of pickup trucks and the presence of French fare like strawberry and raspberry crepes made it clear this Princeton was no small town. For good measure, it had a French sister city, Colmar near the Rhine. But two breakfast spots we visited the next days had some small town attributes.

The Carousel on Nassau Street crowded ten tables into a space meant for half that number. It had a steady flow of breakfast traffic including 50 to 80 regulars—professors, grad students, business people, service people and retirees. Until his retirement Pete Carril, the Hall-of-Famer university basketball coach of 29 years, made the Carousel his morning starting place. No doubt Tiger basketball was the subject of conversation when he was present. (Shades of Indiana and Illinois where basketball was part of breakfast talk.)

At the Carousel, plaid shirts, dungarees and baseball caps were not the apparel of choice. Part owner Allan Schwayer waited on us. No order pad. No bill. Just sidle up to the counter and Allan mentally calculated the charge.

Harry's Luncheonette was on Witherspoon Street, a few minutes walk from the University. Its owner, Harry Ververides, graduated from Princeton High School 39 years ago. His father had come to the United

States from Greece about 1917 and operated the establishment as a candy store and soda fountain for years. Harry changed it to a luncheonette. It opened at 5:30 a.m. for some 40 to 50 early bird regulars. We asked Harry if any famous people had eaten there. "Lowell Thomas and Brooke Shields," he replied.

It came as a surprise when Harry told us that Princeton's fire protection was provided by a totally volunteer department, which covered both the Borough and Township. The hook and ladder founded in 1788 was the oldest company. Woodrow Wilson was a member of Mercer Engine Company #3.

The first settlers were Quakers who came in the 1690s "to enjoy their religious principles without molestation." The name "Princeton" or

"Prince-Town" or "Prince's Town" appeared first in 1724. It was generally believed to honor William III, King of England and Prince of Orange of the House of Nassau.

In 1746, the College of New Jersey was chartered and met in Newark. In 1753 Benjamin Franklin printed 8,000 lottery tickets to fund the fledgling institution. Money from some citizens and a gift of 4.5 acres from Nathaniel FitzRandolph enticed it to relocate in Princeton. Three years later in 1756 the first classes were held in the newly built Nassau Hall, then the largest public building in the colonies.

Early structures were situated on a field-like setting. That's how Princeton's grounds became known as its "campus" (the Latin word for field). It became a standard name used by American colleges except for Harvard's Yard. Among Princeton's firsts in athletics were

- Intercollegiate football game in 1869 (Rutgers 6, Princeton 4)
- Collegiate track meet in 1873
- Intercollegiate baseball no-hitter in 1875 (Princeton 3, Yale 0)
- Collegiate golf champion in 1897
- Indoor college hockey rink in 1923
- Televised baseball game in 1939 (Princeton 2, Columbia 1 in 10 innings).

Over the past 250 years, the relationship with the town has not always been smooth. Nevertheless, there was respect and an undeniable co-relationship between them. It was not until 1896 that the college became Princeton University.

On January 3, 1777, Washington's soldiers encountered the British rear guard outside Princeton and defeated them decisively, though the British managed to ravage Nassau Hall. This and earlier victories at Trenton restored public confidence in the fight for independence.

Princeton was the temporary capital of the United States for four months in 1783. News of the Treaty of Paris signing reached the Continental Congress there.

The town made entertainment history on October 30, 1938, a night that created equal measures of embarrassment and disbelief. Orson Welles' *Mercury Theatre on the Air* broadcast a dramatization of H. G. Welles' novel, *War of the Worlds*. Welles used a relatively new format of on-the-scene reporting, and dramatized a Martian space ship landing just four miles from Princeton near Grover's Mill. It was so convincing that a nationwide panic ensued. A number of disclaimers during the program and Orson Welles declaration that it was a Halloween spoof didn't lessen the impact. A few families in this erudite college town actually packed up their station wagons and fled.

The busiest street in the Borough is a section of New Jersey Route 27, commonly known as Nassau Street. It runs approximately east to west with the University on the south side. Undergraduates ventured across the street for a movie, shopping at Woolworth's, a pizza, or a stop at the post office. Off Nassau Street were busy Palmer Square and the Nassau Tavern. The Tavern, better known as "The Nass," was once an undergraduate watering hole.

The Princeton Cemetery "since 1757" was the resting place of university presidents. A towering statue of Paul Tulane stands with his back to the University.

Locals say that Tulane's back was his response to the University's rejection of a substantial monetary offer to the University if it changed its name to his.

On the rainy morning of our departure we visited the Borough Municipal Building for a photo with Mayor Reed by the USS Princeton bell. At the last moment, we decided on coffee and donuts by the Township's Municipal Building to preserve our 32 "Breakfasts in Princeton." Just in case a purist might not count our breakfast in Princeto(w)n, New York.

I would never have predicted when first coming to Princeton as a freshman in the fall of 1946 that 50 years later I would have breakfast with its president after a year of visiting its 31 namesakes. True to a revered University song, "Going Back to Nassau Hall," I had gone back.

"...24,000 Miles, Never Missed Breakfast"

...St. Louis Post-Dispatch column – 5/14/1997

An epilogue.

*S*t. *Louis Post-Dispatch* columnist Bill McClellan wrote a column on May 14, 1997, headlined "Couple Travelled 24,000 Miles, Never Missed Breakfast." It summarized our unusual road trip. (Actually the "official" mileage was 24,093 miles.) In closing, Bill suggested that we visit towns name Perry. There were over 20, but that's for other Perrys to do.

Our odyssey consisted of 12 separate trips from start to finish. We crossed 30 states, and completed the entire journey in 52 days less than a year. We had accomplished something no one else had attempted, nor was likely to do. The weather varied from harshly cold and snowy to pleasantly warn and sunny.

We ate in local cafes, under street signs, in front of and in post offices, in an inn and in private homes. Our breakfasts ranged from coffee and donuts (9 times) to standard breakfast fare to crepes aux fraise et aux framboises. A dozen newspapers interviewed us.

We visited towns, villages and mere crossroads that had a common name. Some were well past their "glory days." Some were struggling, or had been absorbed by larger neighboring communities. Some were satisfied with the status quo, and some were prosperous. As anticipated, we learned much about the history of our country from its eastern infancy to its western growth. But the itineraries, the histories, and the real estate were secondary. The unexpected reward was touching and being touched by the human part of each community. There were truly welcoming and caring people in Princeton.

Which Princeton did we most like? The one we were in, of course.

Which breakfast did we most enjoy? The one we were eating, of course.

Appendix

"The Roads Less Travelled."
"Old and young, large and small"
"What's in a name?"
"While the tiger stands defender...."
"Grits, ships, haircut...and others"

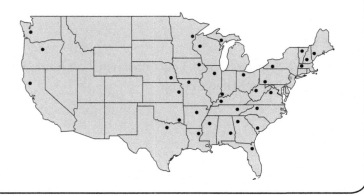

"The Roads Less Travelled."

1996 Princeton Trips by Month

Trip 1   January 29-February 1 by car from St. Louis
Missouri
Nebraska
Kansas

Trip 2   February 14-16 by car from St. Louis
Indiana
Kentucky

Trip 3   March 18-22 by car from St. Louis
Arkansas
Louisiana
Texas

Trip 4   April 13-20 by air from St. Louis, then rental car from San Francisco
California, San Mateo County
California, Colusa County
Oregon
Idaho

Trip 5   May 13-16 by car, en route from St. Louis to Rockport, MA
Ohio (with two kitties)
Pennsylvania
New York

Trip 6   June 6 by car, from Rockport, MA
Massachusetts

Trip 7   July 8-9 by car from Rockport, MA
Maine

Trip 8   July 23-26 by car, en route from Rockport to St. Louis
Illinois
Iowa

Trip 9   August 12-16 by car, en route from St. Louis to Rockport, MA
Wisconsin
Minnesota
Michigan

Trip 10   October 13-18 by car, Rockport, MA to St. Louis
Maryland
North Carolina
West Virginia
Tennessee

Trip 11   November 11-20 by car from St. Louis
Alabama
Georgia (Rockdale County)
Georgia (Clarke County)
South Carolina
Florida (by air, Atlanta to Miami, then rental car)

Trip 12   December 3-7 by air from St Louis, then rental car from Baltimore
to New Jersey

The 1993 Buick Century went to 26 of the 32 Princetons.
There were three flights and three rental cars.
Total mileage: 24,093
Total mileage by car: 16,868

On our business cards, the back showed all the Princetons, except New Jersey, with black dots. New Jersey's was an orange dot.

"Old and young, large and small"

...Statistics

Oldest: New Jersey (1724)

Youngest: Maryland (1940)

Largest: New Jersey (Pop. 12,100)

Smallest: Nebraska (Pop. 30)

Highest Altitude: Oregon (4,111 feet above sea level)

Lowest Altitude: Florida (9.84 feet above sea level)

Easternmost: Maine (67.5722° W)

Southernmost: Florida (25.5384° N)

Westernmost: California – San Mateo (37.5050° W)

Northernmost: Idaho (46.9138° N)

Princetonians

In the early 1990s, over 80,000 people lived in communities named Princeton. Only 9,000 lived in Harvards and 5,000 lived in Yales. (This doesn't count students enrolled at the universities of the same names.)

"What's in a name?"
--early English Playwright

Source of town name by state:

Alabama: For early settlers named Prince

Arkansas: By citizens' petition, possibly because the name had the "flavor of royalty" and honored William, Prince of Orange

California (Colusa): Unknown, although Dr. Almon Lull for reasons unknown "inserted" the name Princeton on petition for a post office

California (San Mateo): Perhaps for "Prince," founder Frank P. Brophy's dog

Florida: For the University by mill owner Gaston "Duck" Drake, Class of 1894

Georgia (Clarke): For the Prince family, first owners of the mill on the site

Georgia (Rockdale): Believed for early Prince family

Idaho: For Princeton, New Jersey, hometown of Orville Clough, a prominent lumberman who gave the school site

Illinois: For Princeton University, school of town Trustee John Musgrove, whose choice was drawn in three-way lottery

Indiana: For Captain William Prince, one of four original county commissioners whose lot was drawn

Iowa: Unknown, but a historian wrote that "Princeton" seemed to have been a popular name in 1845 when the town was founded

Kansas: For Princeton, IL, hometown of settler E. M. Peck, who used it when asked for a railroad billing address

Kentucky: For Revolutionary War Captain William Prince whose estate gave 50 acres for public use and streets

Louisiana: By Dolly McCade Prince, wife of plantation owner John Wilson Prince, who said, "Princeton is a pretty name."

Maine: By its third settler, Ebenezer Rolfe, in honor of Princeton, MA, where he was born

Maryland: Unknown. Perhaps from "Prince" in Prince George's County, or by property owners with a Princeton connection

Massachusetts: For Reverend Thomas Prince, Boston's Old South Church pastor, who owned more than 3,000 acres there

Michigan: Generally accepted folklore says an engineer with the Cleveland (Mining) Company named it for his university.

Minnesota: For lumberman John S. Prince, who owned most of the land on the northern part of town

Missouri: For the Revolutionary War Battle of Princeton

Nebraska: By Trustee John Musgrove, winner of a three-way draw He first settled in Princeton, NJ, and later lived Princeton, IL.

New Jersey: Generally believed in honor of William III, King of England and Prince of Orange of the House of Nassau

New York: For John Prince, a state assemblyman and local merchant

North Carolina: By a man who came from Princeton, NJ (and the absence of any Boons, the original settlers)

Ohio: Unknown. Possibly by settlers from Essex County, NJ, near Princeton; nearby Trenton may be from the New Jersey city.

Oregon: By C. B. Smith for his childhood home of Princeton, MA

Pennsylvania: By John Randolph, who laid out the village, for his father's natal city, Princeton, NJ

South Carolina: By a Mrs. Humber who thought that Triangle was not sophisticated enough

Tennessee: When a new school was completed in 1876, teacher Noah Sherfey's little sister proposed Princeton after the university.

Texas: For Prince Dowlen, landowner and promoter of the town

West Virginia: Chosen to recognize the battle in which native son General Hugh Mercer was mortally wounded

Wisconsin: Probably for Princeton, IL, by Henry B. Treat, brother of the founder

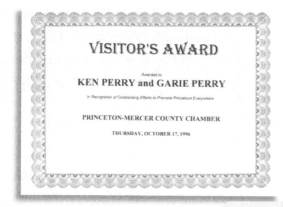

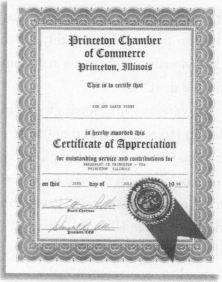

"While the tiger stands defender...."

—University fight song

Team Colors

In 1868, a faculty resolution permitted College of New Jersey students to wear orange ribbons imprinted with "Princeton." The first recorded use of the color orange had been the year before when the Class of 1869 Base Ball Club wore it with black. The College "officially" adopted the two colors in 1877.

Mascots

The tiger was unofficially adopted as the mascot in the 1880s. It was due in part to the popularity of the orange and black colors. Though Harvard's mascot, John Harvard, The Pilgrim, was adopted in 1875, the Princeton tiger could probably lay claim as the oldest animal mascot, and obviously much more ferocious than John. (Yale's bulldog first appeared in 1889.)

The various Princeton high schools had mascots ranging from tigers to loggers to red bugs. Ten of the 32 were tigers. Three (Georgia, North Carolina, Ohio) were bulldogs, also Yale's mascot. The Princeton fight song proclaims: *"While the tiger stands defender of the orange and the black,"* but only one tiger (in Princeton, Minnesota) defended the orange and black. Three (Illinois, Missouri, New Jersey) defended Yale's blue and white. One (Indiana) defended Cornell's red and white. The others defended an assortment of colors.

"Grits, ships, haircut ...and others"

—loose ends

Grits: Southern breakfast and grits go together. A Princeton class-mate and lawyer, Don Cohn, was in New Orleans for some weeks on a legal matter. Each morning, his waitress at the hotel would ask, "Mr. Cohn, you having grits this morning?" To which Don replied, "No thank you." When asked the daily question about grits the day before his return to New York, Don relented. "Yes, bring me a grit."

Ships: Six U. S. Navy ships have sailed as the USS Princeton. The first was commissioned in 1843. The latest is a Ticonderoga-class guided missile cruiser upon which we had breakfast with the captain.

Haircut: A 60s crew cut with short bangs was called "A Princeton."

Pie: We would definitely return to two Princetons for their pies. Maine and Ohio.

Postcards: The 32 cards sent to President Shapiro are in the archives of the Seeley G. Mudd Manuscript Library at Princeton University.

Merger: After four attempts and 60 years, the Borough of Princeton and Princeton Township merged on January 1, 2013.

U.S. 1: From Princeton, Maine, drive 2,086 miles south on U.S. 1 and you will reach Princeton, Florida.

Canada: There are three Princetons, in Newfoundland, Ontario, British Columbia.

Others: Princeton Glacier (Alaska), Mt. Princeton (Colorado) and abandoned cattle railroad loading site (Colorado).

"Tyger! Tyger!"

About the Author

Ken Perry (of course!) graduated from Princeton University, class of 1950 and earned a B.S. degree in chemical engineering. He lettered in cross-country and was elected to Phi Beta Kappa. He worked at Monsanto Company in production and management for 32 years.

The Perrys have traveled beyond Princetons in the U.S., having visited three Princetons in Canada, and Princetowns in England and Hawaii. They have been to 75 countries and all seven continents.

They have been on 11 Elderhostel/Road Scholar programs and six Earthwatch studies. They have long been involved with international students. For 37 years, Garie Perry has taught ESL to adult newcomers from about 40 countries at the International Institute of St. Louis.

Ken and Garie taught English in China for one year. They directed a summer program there for eight years, teaching ESL to Chinese teachers of English.

The Perrys have lived in suburban St. Louis County since 1969. A family summer home in Rockport, MA, keeps them out of the St. Louis heat for five months each year.

They enjoy church involvement, reading, crossword puzzles, jigsaw puzzles, and Joshua, their cat. Ken still plays tennis and writes Class of '50 Notes for the *Princeton Alumni Weekly*. Garie does aerobics and collects owls. And, of course, they both enjoy going out to breakfast.

CPSIA information can be obtained
at www.ICGtesting.com
Printed in the USA
BVOW07*0136010616

450290BV00001B/1/P